JB JOSSEY-BASS™
A Wiley Brand

Media Relations for Nonprofits

115 Winning Ideas to Improve Your Media Relations Efforts

Scott C. Stevenson, Editor

WILEY

978-1-118-69300-1   ISBN

978-1-118-70442-4   ISBN (online)

Media Relations for Nonprofits

115 Winning Ideas
To Improve Your Media Relations Efforts

Published by

Stevenson, Inc.

P.O. Box 4528 • Sioux City, Iowa • 51104
Phone 712.239.3010 • Fax 712.239.2166
www.stevensoninc.com

Media Relations for Nonprofits: 115 Winning Ideas to Improve Your Media Relations Efforts.
Edited by Scott C. Stevenson.
© 2009 Stevenson, Inc. Published 2009 by Stevenson, Inc.

1 Get Media Packets to Those Reporters Who Fail to Attend

When the news media arrives at your press conference, hand each member a media packet. It should contain the following items:

- News release
- News conference agenda
- List of speakers and their bios, resumes and contact information
- Organizational and topic background information
- Printed versions of the speeches or statements
- Photos, CDs or DVDs and a camera-ready version of your logo

Be sure to send a media packet to all media that did not attend; they may still be interested in doing a story. Maintain a list of all media that received the packets and follow up with each of them after the press conference to see if they need any further assistance to publish or produce their story.

2 Four Steps To Handling Negative Publicity

Controversy may never knock on the front door of your organization, but having a procedure for handling possible negative media coverage can help you maintain your focus in a potentially stressful situation — and diffuse misstatements that could add fuel to the fire.

- **Anticipate problems and develop a plan.** Which aspects of your organization might be of interest to the media? Questionable fundraising procedures and misuse of donations or disgruntled contributors are among the possibilities. Your plan of action should outline who will be your organization's official spokesperson, who will coordinate and answer media calls, and who will investigate what went wrong.

- **Take your time responding to questions without stalling.** Bad news may take you by surprise, and you may need to gather much more information before answering reporters. Be forthright and assure them that you will get back to them with a statement. Ask about their deadlines and give them a reasonable timeframe in which they can expect to hear something from you. Keep records of those you have contacted, and those who are still waiting for information. Most news organizations will be as accommodating as they can if they believe you are sincere about getting back to them.

- **Inform key staff and board members.** As quickly as possible, notify staff and directors about the situation.

Press Conference Planning Checklist

Makes sense to follow a checklist for upcoming press conferences. Here's some of what might be included on your checklist:

- ☐ Confirmed participant involvement
- ☐ Location is visually appealing, convenient and easily accessible for the press
- ☐ Location is handicap accessible
- ☐ There is enough parking
- ☐ Alternate location secured in case of bad weather
- ☐ Arranged for site security
- ☐ Audiovisual equipment secured
- ☐ Location has a platform, podium or stage
- ☐ Provided enough lighting
- ☐ There is enough room for cameras
- ☐ Location has good acoustics and/or microphones have been secured
- ☐ There are enough electric outlets (especially close to the platform/stage)
- ☐ Provided enough seating
- ☐ Created a reception area/sign-for the press
- ☐ Sent media advisory out one week prior to event
- ☐ Briefed staff
- ☐ Developed anticipated questions and answers and obtained written statements for the spokesperson
- ☐ Assembled a press kit to hand out at event

When time permits, tell them before they hear about it on the news or read it in the paper. Some may provide valuable advice on how to respond with positive actions to offset the bad news.

- **Follow up with steps to improve community relations.** If apologies are in order, do so graciously and sincerely. Express your organization's willingness to learn from the mistake. Outline specific steps to both repair the damage, and move forward with programs and services to benefit the public.

3 Media Terms

Pitch Letter — Letter to journalist or editor introducing story ideas or other salient information.

Tease — Enticing lead to a story that tells just enough about the story to urge the reader or listener to continue.

4 Get the Entire Production Team on Your Side

Although you may have a primary contact at a particular media outlet, don't underestimate the entire team of people who make up a newspaper, radio station, TV station or other media outlet. Those whose work supports your primary contact person can positively or negatively impact whether your story gets told as well as the manner in which it is delivered to the public — an article's or PSA's placement, timing, amount of editing that takes place once you have submitted the information and more.

Depending on the number of employees or the size of a certain news department, consider a gesture of kindness that

benefits everyone involved. For instance, on a hot summer afternoon, you might pick up an inexpensive foam cooler and fill it with ice and assorted ice cream bars, then drop it off with your contact, asking him/her to share it with the rest of the team.

Inexpensive but thoughtful gestures that show your appreciation such as these will not go unremembered. But they need not, and should not, be done on a regular basis. Too much wooing will only appear that you are attempting to "buy" their loyalty.

5 Create a Top-notch Press Kit

Press kits are an integral part of any organization's marketing plan. They can be distributed in a variety of ways and are one of the most effective tools an organization can use to spread their message.

The Tennessee Aquarium (Chattanooga, TN) makes its press kit available in different ways to accommodate the media. Kathie Scobee Fulgham says, "Our press kits are online and downloadable — as are our photos. When journalists visit or when we do snail mailings, we burn our press kits on a CD and place them in a 'clam shell.'"

Press kits are vital when contacting the media because they provide needed information about your organization's mission and goals. Fulgham says, "Media use press kits as background to form their stories or to spark story ideas of their own. They're able to cut and paste information from electronic press kits to put in their own words, download

photos and compose a top-notch feature or travel story."

Fulgham offers these tips for nonprofits trying to create press kits:

- Keep your press kit up to date.
- It's better to have several short pieces than one or two long pieces.
- Electronic press kits with links to the Web are a plus.
- Always give a quick way to contact a live person.
- At-a-glance pieces are helpful to the media because they save time.
- Get a journalist or panel of journalists to tell you what they think should go in your press kit — stats and quotes from other pubs, for example.

Source: Kathie Scobee Fulgham, Tennessee Aquarium, Chattanooga, TN. Phone (423) 785-3007. E-mail: ksf@tennis.org

6 Reach Out to Media for 'Dream' Coverage

Waiting for that "dream" story (you know... the one that both accurately and emotionally captures the good work your nonprofit organization does) to appear magically in the media? Well, why not take the bull by the horns and take your story to the media?

Invite a few "hand-selected" reporters to your facility and offer them an exclusive "behind-the-scenes" look at your organization. Bringing reporters on site allows you to control the discussion.

Bring them in individually, rather than as a group, and give them a tour of your facility. More importantly, give them access to key programs, departments or individuals (e.g., the CEO or executive director, key researchers, top board members, etc.). Allow time for one-on-one interviews.

Also, be sure to emphasize the aspects you want covered in the story.

You'll find this approach will help yield long-term results.

7 Interview Tip

- If a reporter calls you at a bad time, or when you are unprepared to respond to his/her questions, ask "When is your deadline?" Politely explain that now is not a good time to talk and that you would be happy to call the reporter back at another mutually acceptable time. This gives you a chance to collect your thoughts.

8 How to Get Free PR Expertise

Like many communications directors at nonprofit organizations, you are expected to wear a number of hats in areas that are sometimes outside the realm of your formal expertise.

Your department may not have a budget for hiring outside public relations consultants, but making proper contacts through community networking events may help you develop a "go-to" list of experts who can advise you for little or no cost.

- **Join your local chamber of commerce.** Most of them hold mixing events and membership luncheons where you can meet public relations professionals. Some also offer free or low-cost seminars where owners of public relations firms offer advice.

- **Become involved in organizations complementing your own.** As a volunteer for institutions who do have public relations departments, you may find colleagues who are willing to share ideas.

- **Develop a partnership.** Team up with a public relations firm that seeks an alliance with a nonprofit cause specifically so they can add volunteer activities to their own company resumes. Most public relations firms choose one or two local causes to support with gratis services — convince them that yours should be one of them.

- **Look online for PR firm websites.** Even if you have to wade through websites promising something for nothing to get to the meat, there are plentiful resources for public relations strategies, advice and free subscriptions to e-newsletters.

- **Subscribe to professional journals.** Just because you're not an official public relations professional doesn't mean that you can't buy magazines, journals or newsletters written for them.

- **Ask a PR professional to join your board.** Do some research to see which public relations professionals in your area are most likely to be supportive of your organization's mission. Invite them to have lunch, a tour of your facility and see your programs in action. Ask them how your organization might help increase community awareness of your services and show them specific ways their involvement on your board will be mutually beneficial.

9 When a News Editor Says 'No'

You have a great story. You make the perfect pitch. The timing couldn't be better. And still the news editor or assignment editor turns down your offer to do a story.

What do you do now?

The story doesn't have to be dead in the water. Try one or more of the following suggestions to turn that editor's "no" into a "yes".

✓ **Offer the story at a different time.** All news agencies, be they print or broadcast, have slow news days. Find out from the editor when those slow times usually are and rework the pitch to fit that time line.

✓ **Offer to do the reporter's job for them.** If the news department can't send out a photographer, offer to take the photos and e-mail them with a written report on your event. Make sure to find out any guidelines for required image format and resolution, story length and deadlines.

✓ **Always have a backup.** If the news person doesn't like your first story idea, always have a second one prepared. Just make sure both are truly newsworthy.

✓ **Always have a Plan B.** If the first media entity says no, always have a second one in mind.

10 Get on Agenda For Media's Ascertainment Meetings

Did you know the FCC requires TV and radio stations in each media market to meet four times per year to educate the editors and public service directors on issues of concern in their community?

These are called "ascertainment meetings," and speakers are invited in to do the educating.

You could be one of those speakers, getting your message to representatives from multiple broadcast outlets at once and leading to a more significant relationship with important media contacts.

To get on the agenda, ask your most significant TV or radio contact for information about the local meetings. Meetings generally rotate among various stations in the market.

Also, be sure to plan ahead. Since the meetings are quarterly, the agendas are usually planned well in advance. So if you are planning to pitch a time-specific event you will want to get on board early. Try reaching out at least six months prior to the event.

At the meeting, make your message concise. Ask for something specific (e.g., radio support in the form of PSAs for an upcoming event, a media spokesperson to emcee a gala event, a monthly radio profile of a client). Ambiguous requests like "more support for our programs" force reporters and assignment editors to do the work and come up with an idea of how to do that. You'll be more likely to get a taker if you already have a plan and just need their help to make it happen.

11 Finding Right Spokesperson Key to Strong Media Ties

Identifying and grooming the right person to deal with media inquiries — especially those involving controversial matters — can help your organization maintain solid media relationships.

"Carefully choose who will tell your story to the media and the public," says Kristen Blessman, associate director for media relations, Regis University (Denver, CO). "If you're going to develop good relationships with the media and your public, they have to trust you as an individual PR person and the organization you work for."

Be prepared to seek out the right person to respond to the issue with finesse and expertise, she says.

"A good PR person, upon receiving word that negative information about their organization has made its way to the public, will carefully analyze the information, research its truth and validity, learn the whole story and immediately find the person within their organization with the most knowledge on the topic," says Blessman.

That person may not always be the CEO or PR person, she says.

For instance, she says: "After the Virginia Tech shootings, we were being contacted by several local media outlets wanting to know what we were doing to keep our campus safe. This is a perfect instance where the president of Regis could have been a 'face' man stating the things we had in place to be secure as a campus. However, we had a Regis faculty member who was a police officer for 30 years and could talk about the potential mind-set of the individual who committed the crime.

"In addition, we had an expert on campus who could talk about security on college campuses and had a wealth of knowledge about this topic."

Carefully evaluating media inquiries will help you identify the appropriate staff member to handle the request, she says. "Basically, it's finding who in your organization has the kind of information the media is looking for and being proactive rather than reactive."

Source: Kristen Blessman, Associate Director for Media Relations, Regis University, Denver, CO. Phone (303) 458-4273.

12 Ask Trusted Media Contacts for Input

Wondering which angle to use to promote your story to the media? Consider reaching out to trusted media contacts for their input in developing your pitch.

"Since I made the transition from print journalist to a communications practitioner nearly 10 years ago, there have been several instances where I have contacted trusted media sources to ask their advice on how to respond to a situation or simply how best to promote a specific program or event," says Natasha A. Suber, director of communications, Pfeiffer University (Misenheimer, NC).

When the university made plans to offer a new nursing program, Suber contacted the health editor at the state's largest daily newspaper to ask what would catch her attention and entice her to write a story about the program.

"Our conversation and her advice helped me to prepare talking points and compose responses to anticipated difficult questions our administrators could be asked," Suber says. "The biggest single question the editor prompted us to ask ourselves was: 'How is this program unique?'

"We then took that a step further and asked ourselves: 'What would encourage prospective students to enroll in the Pfeiffer University program over all other similar programs offered?'" says Suber. "These are questions, even as a former reporter, I may not have even thought to ask our administrators."

The health editor also suggested they discuss ways their program could potentially help address the nursing shortage, says Suber, noting: "By seeking a trusted reporter's input from time to time, I know I'm answering the critical questions they would ask."

When deciding which media contacts to reach out to, choose those with whom you have developed a solid working relationship, she says. "I suggest communications professionals identify a reporter who covers their industry and invite them to coffee or lunch. Develop a relationship and find out what stories they enjoy covering, what they think makes a good story and provide those sorts of stories when making pitches.

"Also, get to know their writing style by reading their articles or watching their reports. If they do a great job on a story, send them a note or call them to tell them so."

While getting advice from media contacts can benefit your organization, knowing when not to seek the media's opinion is also important.

"Consider the relationship you have developed," Suber advises. "If it's a reporter you don't know well, they have nothing vested in the relationship and might take what you tell them straight to their editors because they can get a 'scoop' on the story. Also, if the situation is potentially negative and includes personnel issues, etc., you don't want to share that with any reporter, even one you trust.

"Avoid putting any media source in a situation where they have to choose between your friendship/relationship and their job. Remember, they are still looking for the next great story idea — positive or negative. In those situations, speak only to colleagues you can trust if you really need advice."

Source: Natasha A. Suber, Director of Communications, Pfeiffer University, Misenheimer, NC. Phone (704) 463-3040. E-mail: natasha.suber@pfeiffer.edu

13 Highlight Communications Staff Online

Turn the spotlight on your communications staff with a website devoted to your communications department and its services.

At University of California, Davis (Davis, CA), communications staff had developed websites for many campus units, but not for their own department, says Lisa Lapin, assistant vice chancellor, university communications.

"We really are a service unit and we wanted to make it as easy as possible for the people we work with on and off campus to access the many services we provide and to seek our help," says Lapin. So they created a website dedicated to the communications department (http://ucomm.ucdavis.edu).

The 60-page site — with publication resources, staff bios, contact information for media, internal campus communication guidelines and more — took seven months to create. Web staff spend minimal time keeping it up to date.

Susanne Rockwell, university communications web editor, says that before the specialized site was launched, "we didn't really have a site that was central to university communications and nobody knew where to find us."

To spread the word, they sent a mass e-mail to 2,800 media contacts and a separate e-mail to 120 "campus communicators."

The website's goal "was to improve service to our constituents by making it easier for them to get information," Rockwell says. "We accomplished our goal of showing 'service with a personal touch' by initiating staff photos and bios and organizing the whole site to allow people easy access to information and service. We also improved index pages for the media and campus community so people could find what they wanted easily — the one-stop shopping idea."

The site was also designed with staff in mind, she says. "We wanted to offer to our internal folks a rational approach to news priorities and communicate guidelines to the campus by posting a matrix with guidelines for news, honors and events publicity. It is amazing how people more easily understand and accept our judgment when we can show them a matrix with a well-thought-out chart of how we measure how to treat various news stories."

For organizations who plan to highlight communications staff online, Rockwell advises: "Get your office involved and explain why having their photos and professional information on the Web is a good thing (because it gives them credibility). Don't make pages that are hard to update. If you have a lot of turnover and problems keeping software programmers, it is tough to update the bio files."

Sources: Susanne Rockwell, University Communications Web Editor; Lisa Lapin, Assistant Vice Chancellor, University Communications, University of California, Davis, Davis, CA. Phone (530) 752-9842.

Content not available in this edition

Content not available in this edition

Providing easy-to-navigate links to key information (top page) and biographies and contact information for staff (above) were two goals that University of California, Davis staff had in mind when they created a website especially to spotlight their communications department.

Communications Website, by the Numbers

Rockwell shares these statistics regarding its communications department website:

- 23,326 unique visitors over 12 months (Nov. 16, 2006 through Nov. 16, 2007) looking at 72,000 pages for an average of 2.6 pages per visitor.

- Average of 200 page views a day to this 60-page site.

- About 42 percent of visitors arrive at site via search engine.

- Almost 40 percent of visitors are internal.

14 Get on Radio Talk Shows

Radio can be overlooked as a viable medium when seeking publicity for your organization.

While newspaper, television and even Internet exposure can be very important for increasing awareness of your mission, radio interviews can help you reach out to thousands at a time in a more personal way.

How can you become a radio guest on popular programs in your community? These guidelines can help you get started:

- **Be a listener first.** Regularly tune in to the most talked-about radio programs in your area, getting familiar with the host, format, favorite topics, regular callers and the audience. When you approach a host to appear on his or her program, knowing the specifics of their formats will add credibility when you explain why you would be an appropriate guest.

- **Be a caller.** If the format is call-in and you hear a topic that you feel fully confident in addressing as an expert in your field, explain to the screener who you are, your organization and the points you can add to the current issue. Weekday mornings are the peak time to be heard.

15 Develop a 'Testimonial Type' Checklist

Testimonials can prove powerful in any number of ways: attracting customers, enhancing public perception of your organization, inviting financial contributions and sponsorships, recruiting volunteers and more.

To make the most of testimonials, develop a checklist of sources to whom you can go for testimonials. Here's a more generic list you can use to develop one that best fits your organization:

_____ Current and/or former customers

_____ Current and/or former employees

_____ Vendors

_____ City, state or national leaders

_____ Celebrities

_____ Donors

_____ Volunteers

_____ Persons from certain professions

_____ Members of the media

_____ Individuals based on age (youth, seniors)

_____ Individuals based on geographic preferences

- **Promote your availability.** Send radio hosts e-mails, hand-written notes or phone them to make an informal introduction. Mention topics discussed on their shows in each contact, and be prepared to continue the process over several months until they are well aware of who you are, the organization you represent and your credentials as a spokesperson.

- **Always be forthright.** If you or someone from your organization is chosen to be a "guest expert" on any topic for broadcast, make sure you can deliver the gravitas the host expects and the subject deserves. Failure to do so can have embarrassing consequences for you and your institution.

- **Flexibility for last-minute appearances.** When previously scheduled guests have conflicts, radio hosts are left with gaps to fill. Volunteer in advance to be an emergency substitute with several pre-selected topics involving aspects of your organization, such as "Healthy After School Snacks" if you represent a food bank, or "Creating Your Own First-Aid Kit" if you're in the health care field.

16 Be Proactive With Media Outreach

Being proactive is essential when trying to get an important story heard by the media.

"We have built strong relationships with local media by being proactive and not just reactive," says Cary Rentola, marketing, community outreach and volunteer program manager, Larimer Humane Society (Fort Collins, CO). "If we have a unique story about an adoption or rescue or we need the community's help in an animal cruelty case, we send out a press release. I make sure I'm prepared to answer requests for interviews as they come. In being proactive, we established ourselves as a resource for animal care. If the local media is working on an animal care piece, we regularly are contacted as a resource or for more information."

Taking a proactive stance with the media can make a major difference when trying to garner attention for newsworthy items. It also helps to create name recognition with local media outlets and develop relationships with reporters. "In order to maintain the relationships we have, I keep an updated media distribution list with contact information. This allows me to send press releases and other information out quickly and reach all types of media including television, print and radio. Through our work, positive image and professional response, we have also gained in-kind media sponsorships for events and partnerships to spotlight adoptable animals," Rentola says.

Source: Cary Rentola, Marketing, Community Outreach and Volunteer Program Manager, Larimer Humane Society, Fort Collins, CO. E-mail: cary@larimerhumane.org

17 Appeal to National Media

Think national media exposure is out of reach? Think again. Rather than being intimidated by the prospect of approaching the national media, look within your organization for a story angle that appeals to a nationwide audience.

Hosting an event that draws national interest is one way to get national attention, says Gary Stromberg, head of The BLACKBIRD Group (Westport, CT) and public relations representative, Silver Hill Hospital (New Canaan, CT). "The other route is to find an angle or story idea that resonates."

For instance, Stromberg recently pitched a story about Silver Hill to Forbes magazine.

"Silver Hill was desirous of national media exposure but recognized the improbability of that happening," he says. "I was kicking around the idea of the uniqueness of Silver Hill as one of only a handful of independent psychiatric hospitals when it occurred to me that Forbes might be a good publication to pitch. This was based on working with them in the past and a relationship I've developed with one of their senior business editors."

Stromberg e-mailed the story idea to his Forbes connection, and the senior editor decided to pursue the story.

"Senior editors have this authority where more junior editors would have to obtain approval before proceeding," he notes. "I next arranged for him to visit the hospital, tour the facility and interview several key administrators. He is now working up a first draft of his article and will let me know if he requires anything further of me or the staff at Silver Hill."

Identifying and successfully pitching a story to the national media is a challenge that — in many cases — requires the experience, know how and imagination of a good publicist, Stromberg says. "The best advice I can give is to decide what publication you'd like to be in, read and understand that publication, find the appropriate editor to approach, then come up with a pitch you think will be of interest."

Source: Gary Stromberg, Head of The BLACKBIRD Group; PR Representative, Silver Hill Hospital, Westport, CT. Phone (203) 221-8100. E-mail: gary.stromberg@gmail.com

18 A Day in the Life of a Media Relations Director

A daily journal can be a highly effective tool to track challenges and accomplishments and chart your ongoing progress. Here's a day in the life of Richard Relkin, director of media relations, St. Francis College (Brooklyn Heights, NY):

Oct. 17, 2007:

9-9:30 a.m.: Put finishing touches on media release (right) concerning SFC Alerts, the college's emergency notification system. Send release to vice president and president for final approval.

9:30-10:30 a.m.: Work with students at sign-up booth for SFC Alerts to help them enter text message, instant message and cell phone information and make sure system is working properly before sending release to media.

11 a.m.-noon: Receive approval and send out SFC Alerts release. Upload release to run live online. Make other changes and updates to various sections of the website which relaunched two days previously.

1:30-2 p.m.: Edit monthly calendar card of college events mailed to area senior citizens.

2-3 p.m.: Write release for media calendars to list upcoming event, Leslie Bennetts talking about The Feminine Mistake.

3-4 p.m.: Attend planning meeting for events and communication strategies for college's 150th anniversary.

4:30 p.m.: Confirm plans for NBC News affiliate's reporter/videographer to attend tomorrow's men's water polo match.

Source: Richard Relkin, Director of Media Relations, St. Francis College, Brooklyn Heights, NY. Phone (718) 489-5214. E-mail: rrelkin@stfranciscollege.edu

Content not available in this edition

19 Create Online Media Archive

An online media archives section can provide easy, 24-hour access to valuable information, as well as a brief snapshot into your organization's recent history.

Officials at Calvin College (Grand Rapids, MI) began an online media archives section about 10 years ago.

"We started putting our releases on the Web in the summer of 1997 and at the end of a year we figured we might as well keep on going with it," says Phil de Haan, director of media relations. "We wanted to keep the current school year as the most easily viewed but also make old releases available via the archives."

The more inclusive your media archive is, the more likely users are to find the information they seek.

"We wanted to make our releases available to wider audiences and we wanted to maintain an archive where people could go back and look at what was posted," says de Haan. "In this day and age of Google searches, it becomes even more valuable to have a historical archive out there for people to peruse."

The site draws persons in, he says, citing e-mails from persons wanting to know more about a speaker Calvin College hosted in an on-campus project.

When determining how far back to go with an archives section, consider the effort involved, de Haan says. "Either go back to the beginning or begin now and create the structure for an archive going forward. Adding news releases after the fact can be a lot of work."

But, he says, the work is worthwhile.

"A well-maintained news archives section provides a college's many audiences with a good sense of what the place is all about," de Haan says. For instance, a prospective student "can read about new majors that were added, student papers published in prestigious journals, an annual international student talent show, the cardboard canoe contest and much more."

Announce the creation of your archives section, as well as milestones, such as its five- or 10-year anniversary, to remind media and others of the useful information available on your website.

Source: Phil de Haan, Director of Media Relations, Calvin College, Grand Rapids, MI. Phone (616) 526-6475. E-mail: dehp@calvin.edu

20 How to Be Sure Your Media Advisory Gets Attention

Brief and to the point, media advisories can garner significant attention while respecting editors' time constraints and communication professionals' efforts.

Like press releases though, advisories can also get overlooked.

Cole Krawitz is communication strategist for SPIN Project (San Francisco, CA). SPIN's mission is to strengthen nonprofit social justice organizations to communicate effectively for themselves by providing accessible and affordable strategic communications consulting, training, coaching, networking opportunities and concrete tools.

To make sure your press releases and advisories make it past the editor's desk to the assignment desk, Krawitz advises, incorporate these four factors:

1. A clear indication of camera-friendly visuals built into the event.

2. A punchy, direct headline and lead paragraph establishing newsworthiness with clear news hooks.

3. Information stating if advisory is for immediate release or to be held until set date.

4. Information on how to reach at least two points of contact for the event.

What shouldn't your advisory contain? Jargon, acronyms or policy speak, the communications strategist says.

Source: Cole Krawitz, Communication Strategist, SPIN Project, San Francisco, CA. Phone (415) 227-4200. E-mail: info@spinproject.org

21 Use National News to Your Advantage

Tying your agency's mission to national news can mean great local coverage.

Always keep an eye out for ways to connect the agency's services, staff and clients to bigger stories and trends. When you find a match, contact reporters.

Reporters and editors are always looking for ways to localize a major story. One agency had a client with a walk-on role in a major motion picture. When the movie opened, every local TV affiliate wanted an interview with that client.

Helping a reporter or editor in this way can build a relationship that will benefit your organization in the future. It also helps generate awareness of your organization with an audience that you may not have reached otherwise.

22 Learn New Media Tools Before Offering Them to Others

When creating a news-related Web page or revamping your old news page, familiarize yourself with new technologies to ensure you are incorporating the right features.

Recent updates to the website for Swarthmore College (Swarthmore, PA) incorporate the latest technology, says Alisa Giardinelli, associate director of news and information, communications office.

"There was an old news site that served us well, but we wanted to do more. We share the desire to showcase, in a more interactive and dynamic way, the energy and variety of life on campus. Whether it is a Taiko drumming lesson or a lecture on planet formation, in a classroom or on a stage, we want to show in as many ways as possible how life at Swarthmore supports and enriches the life of the mind."

Time spent educating yourself on new media technologies, as well as what other like-minded organizations are incorporating into their news sites, will assist you in the design process and provide you with an arsenal of information.

In the case of Swarthmore's update, "We did some benchmarking of comparable sites and educated ourselves about new media in various ways just to make sure we were on the right track," says Giardinelli.

Benchmarking efforts included participating in a new media workshop organized by the Public Relations Society of America (PRSA); a Bacon's/PRSA webinar; a PRSA teleseminar for counselors to higher education on the topic, "The Latest Web Trends for Colleges and Universities," and a CASE-sponsored teleseminar: "How New Media is Changing the Face of University Relations."

The efforts proved beneficial in helping Swarthmore staff create the new site, she says, noting: "They were very useful in orienting us to the landscape and vocabulary of new media."

In additions, a student employed by the news office researched a dozen college news websites, she says. "The student worker surveyed and reported on how new media is used on a number of college and university sites around the country. She identified the features she liked and offered her candid opinions about them."

"Become a user of the kinds of media you want to employ."

Swarthmore staff launched the updated news site in early spring 2008, creating it in-house through a collaborative effort between the news and information office, media services, alumni relations and the information technology department. The new site (www.swarthmore.edu/news) contains videos, podcasts, RSS feeds and blogs.

In determining what to change about the online news page, they considered carefully what they wanted to stay the same, Giardinelli says.

"We wanted to keep the best parts of the current site and freshen them up a bit — our sources and experts, news headlines and flagship publications," she says.

Exploring new media technologies first hand is the best way to determine which features will be the most beneficial and effective for your website. "The best advice is to become a user of the kinds of media you want to employ," says Giardinelli. "Short of that, talk — and listen — to people who do."

Source: Alisa Giardinelli, Associate Director of News and Information, Communications Office, Swarthmore College, Swarthmore, PA. Phone (610) 690-5717. Website: www.swarthmore.edu/news

23 Make a Good First Impression Via Phone

To make a good first impression with someone using the phone:

1. Think about what it is you want to accomplish before placing the call.

2. After introducing yourself, ask "Is this a good time to talk?" If it's not, set a phone appointment.

3. Put a smile in your voice. Several studies have indicated that a high percentage of phone contacts make decisions on the tone of a person's voice rather than the actual words that were shared.

24 Looking for Media Coverage? Be Proactive

If your organization is looking to increase your media exposure, be proactive and reach out to the local publications in your area that cover nonprofit happenings to let them know you are available for interviews.

Many cities and towns produce their own free monthly or quarterly publications detailing happenings in the area, events and other news. Staff with independent newspapers and other smaller publications may also be more inclined to write a story about your organization, or let you write your own feature than would be those at more mainstream publications.

Search online for publications in your area and be sure to check with your local chamber of commerce for an updated listing. In addition, you can find many local free publications in diners, hotels and other local establishments. Become familiar with these publications and make a list of those you feel may be interested in your events and programs before contacting them.

25 Major Announcement? Consider Hosting a Media Day

A media day allows you to invite a large number of local media to your facilities and provide an ideal platform to share an important announcement or development.

Dan Jorgensen, former director of public relations and assistant to the president currently serving as adjunct professor for journalism and public relations courses at Augsburg College, (Minneapolis, MN) explains:

"We held a media day to announce a major new scholarship program, Scholastic Connections, to serve students of color and to help offset a hurtful racist letter-writing campaign by one of our alumni. As we learned more about what our alum had been doing, there was a strong sense that something needed to be done in response and that we should create a positive response."

That response? Hosting a media day focused on creating a positive situation out of a hurtful series of events. Specifically, college officials organized the media day to show the media that:

1. While one alum was obviously racist in his attitudes and actions, the college itself was far from it, and faculty and staff were working tirelessly to prove so.

2. The student body was very diverse and students of color were treated with dignity and respect, and playing key leadership roles on campus.

3. Staff and faculty were striving to find ways to make the student body even more diverse, and setting up the Scholastic Connections fund to provide scholarship support and alumni mentors to students of color was a crucial step in that process.

"The Scholastic Connections program was created as a counter to the hurtful things our alum had been doing, and it was officially announced to the media when they came to campus," says Jorgensen. "Because of the lightning-rod effect created by our alum, there was a lot of interest by the media in getting lots of questions answered. Having a day like this gave them an 'open' campus in which to meet the president and minority neighborhood leaders who came to join in and talk about their relationship with the college, and to talk freely with students and faculty about their experiences."

Augsburg's media day, held in 2001, led to extensive media coverage by four TV stations, public and news radio stations, major newspapers plus several community and minority newspapers including the Metro Lutheran newspaper. Coverage led to two national stories — one by the Associated Press and one by The Chronicle of Higher Education — which, Jorgensen says, "gave Augsburg high marks for the Scholastic Connections program and the college's response to our alum."

A committee spent a month planning the media day, says Jorgensen.

"The committee was made up of the media/PR team and several other staff in the Department of Public Relations and Communication. We also had a couple of alumni, including Syl Jones, whose idea it was to create Scholastic Connections. Syl conducted the opening press briefing and was also available to talk about the issues."

If considering a media day, he says: "Don't be restrictive in where the media can go and what they can do. If you're inviting them to your organization's facilities, make them feel at home and let them talk to people openly and candidly."

Source: Dan Jorgensen, Former Director of Public Relations & Assistant to the President; Judy Petree, Media Relations Manager; Augsburg College, Minneapolis, MN. Phone (612) 330-1176. E-mail: jorgensd@augsburg.edu or petree@augsburg.edu

---

Media Day Details to Consider

Planning a media day to familiarize news persons with your facility and/or make a major announcement? Consider these factors, advises Dan Jorgensen of Augsburg College (Minneapolis, MN):

✓ Where and how can media be 'home-based' for the day?

✓ Do you have a conference room, classroom, small office or other place where they can work on their stories?

✓ Do you have food and drink readily available for them?

✓ Do you have people ready to help guide the media and get them sources and interviews?

---

26 Tips for Responding to Reporters

The media help you do your job by transferring information and generating interest in your organization. However, the way you interact with reporters can affect how clearly and accurately your story gets across. Here are some tips for dealing with reporters:

- **Never say "No comment."** If you don't have accurate information on a topic, explain that. If you have information you can't share, explain why it would be inappropriate for you to answer the question. Remember, if an interview goes in a direction you don't like, you have the right to terminate it.

- **Be leery of speaking off the record.** Don't say something to a reporter if you don't want it to appear in print or be broadcast.

27 Make the Most of 'Awareness' Month

Every organization is governed by an "awareness month" and your name should be out in a bigger than normal way during that period.

Tie in this theme month to a current event or time of year, says Leza Raffel, president, The Communication Solutions Group (Jenkinstown, PA). For example, her company works with the Attention Deficit Disorder Association and in January, they promote Organize Your Desk Month.

Position your organization as an expert on current events and have a source at your organization available for radio interviews.

"The key is to keep your eyes on the news," Raffel says. Listen to what people are talking about and watch what celebrities are doing in the news. News can't wait. If you hear news that ties into your organization in the morning, a press release and other media contacts should be out your door as soon as possible.

Post press releases on your organization's website that your members can tailor to their news and promote in their area. "This becomes a great member benefit," Raffel says.

To gain national and international exposure, post your expert sources at ProfNet (www.profnet.com) and press releases at www.prnewswire.com. You also can watch for reporter requests at ProfNet for sources who match your organization's expertise.

Source: Leza Raffel, President, The Communication Solutions Group, Jenkinstown, PA. Phone (215) 884-6499. E-mail: comsol@comsolutionsgroup.com

28 Organize Media Contact Lists

Allow the media to contact your staff members with ease by creating a media contact list divided by topic.

By listing appropriate staff members by topic, you'll enable the media to quickly browse your site and contact the appropriate person. This is not only beneficial to media contacts but to your staff because it will eliminate media inquiries directed to the wrong person.

If you visit the website of the United States Council for Internal Business (USCIB), www.uscib.org/index.asp, you'll notice its media contact list contains more than 30 topics, with some staff members covering multiple topics. "We find listing our experts by topic helps put beat reporters directly in touch with someone who may know a lot more about an issue than our president, another senior representative or I would," says Jonathan Huneke, vice president of communications.

"We find providing the media with a lot of basic information and contacts up front helps ensure when they do need to reach us, they're not making a stab in the dark and already appreciate how our perspective may add value to their story."

Another benefit to a detailed list of media topics is it aids in developing a solid relationship between your staff and media contacts by providing a consistent, knowledgeable contact person. Huneke says one of the reasons the USCIB decided to list its contacts by topic was to get greater recognition for the individual staff experts, so they can cultivate relationships with reporters working on their issue.

Source: Jonathan Huneke, Vice President, Communications, United States Council for International Business (USCIB), New York, NY. Phone (212) 703-5043. E-mail: jhuneke@uscib.org

29 Update Media Points to Boost Response Time, Accuracy

Ever wonder where a reporter got information about your organization? Want to make sure information reported about your organization is always accurate?

Media points can help.

A quick one-pager listing updated statistical and financial information about your organization can streamline the interview and submission process.

What to include: Current factual and statistical information, including number of people served in the prior year, demographic makeup of those served, number of volunteers, number of board members, cents per dollar raised used towards program services, etc. Include mission statement, eligibility information, purpose statement (if applicable), number of years in operation and recent milestones.

When to use: Include this versatile document in media kits, with press releases, when being interviewed and in your online pressroom to give reporters a resource, and broadcast reporters and anchors accurate talking points.

Of course, it goes without saying that media points should always be up to date. When any change is made, e-mail the updated version to staff, board members and pertinent volunteers, asking them to keep the current version and replace any prior versions.

30 Tips for Better Interviews

Interviewing skills are an important part of your media relations package. Quality interviews determine how the media perceives your organization, and a well-conducted, professional interview can lead to future positive publicity about your organization.

Charles Margulis, media coordinator, Center for Environmental Health, Center for Food Safety (Oakland, CA), details strategies for better media interviews:

1. **Be available.** "It sounds obvious, but it's most important that reporters can easily reach a live person when they call your organization. Your voice mail should include a cell number where you can be reached at any time. Staff who answer phones should be trained to deal with press calls. They can put reporters to voice mail if the reporter indicates that he/she is not on deadline, and that voice mail is acceptable. Also, if you can't talk to a reporter right away, or if you need to research an answer to a question, you must know the reporter's deadline. Instruct your staff to obtain this vital information."

2. **Know their beat/format.** "Most print reporters need stories that fit their area, so tailor your conversation to the reporter's beat. For radio or TV talk show interviews, try to find out the format in advance. Is it one-on-one, or will there be a debate or discussion with other guests? How long is the segment? Also, find out something about the show, its host and demographics, so you can tailor your message and tone appropriately."

3. **Pitch local angles to local reporters.** "Local TV stations and newspapers are still main information sources for most people. Many stories have local angles that can be highlighted. For example, when the Center for Environmental Health exposed lead-tainted baby bibs, we called Chicago reporters to let them know that a Chicago-area grandmother helped us identify the problem. The piece became the lead story for several local network newscasts and was covered by major Chicago newspapers."

4. **Have a single, straightforward message ready.** "For a print reporter or prerecorded interview for TV or radio, you may only get a single, brief soundbite or quote in the final story. You must have your single most important message ready. Craft this message in advance, use it early in the interview and keep coming back to it."

5. **Offer contact information for other sources.** "After doing an interview, especially for an investigative reporter or someone working on a longer time frame, I always offer reporters names of other sources they can talk to for their story. I have ready contact information for colleagues who work on the same issue, including academicians, government officials and other organizations we work with. If your contacts help their story, reporters will keep you in mind as a resource."

Source: Charles Margulis, Media Coordinator, Center for Environmental Health, Center for Food Safety, Oakland, CA

31 Consider a Media Buyer

Using a professional media buyer to design your media plan can dramatically increase your exposure.

The New Jersey Credit Union League (Hightstown, NJ) turned to a media buyer after the ad agency they were using raised fees by 30 percent. Armed with a colleague's referral, Sharon Dilling, director of marketing and communications, reached out to a media buyer.

"This buyer really impressed me," says Dilling. "We have a small ad budget in a big market. She made numerous suggestions and could explain why.... She asked questions about our needs and talked about outlets and options."

The league had $140,000 budgeted for a media buyer. "We agreed to let her design a plan for an hourly fee," Dilling explains. "If we used her buy, she would credit us for the fee and reduce the cost of the buy. If not, we paid only for the plan. Her presentation included information on her experience, philosophy, a detailed scope of her work and what we could expect each step of the way.

"Because our market (New York-Pennsylvania) is the most expensive in the nation," she says, "we needed a

professional who knew how it worked and could work on such a small scale. You can use an agency that uses a buyer, but you're just adding another layer. It's cheaper without the extra overhead."

Dilling says the media buyer suggested ways to maximize exposure on a tight budget, such as sponsoring an event created by a radio station, which will place them in print ads "in places we'd never otherwise appear. Plus, we're getting more air time as a result."

The media buyer also provided a grid for easy reference. It places media buys in time frames that coincide with events. "It's easy to understand, and we intend to distribute it to our members so they can be involved with the campaign when it airs," she says.

When working with a media buyer, says Dilling, ask for references, have a firm budget and define both your message and target audience in advance.

Source: Sharon Dilling, Director of Marketing & Communications, New Jersey Credit Union League, Hightstown, NJ.
E-mail: Sharon.dilling@touro.edu

32 Partnerships Help Strengthen Media Relationships

To strengthen relationships with specific media outlets, find community partners with connections to the outlets you are pursuing to create a mutually beneficial partnership.

To nurture connections with the Spanish-speaking community, staff with The University of California, Los Angeles (UCLA) partnered with the Hispanic Public Relations Association (HPRA) to host professional development seminars on campus.

"Effective media relations work is about building and maintaining relationships," says Phil Hampton, UCLA assistant director of media relations. "Cosponsoring events with HPRA is one of many methods utilized by the UCLA office of media relations to bolster relationships with journalists in the Spanish-speaking news media."

Letisia Marquez, UCLA senior media relations officer and HPRA scholarship chair, helped facilitate two seminars that included workshops, panel discussions and mixers. Most planning was done by phone and e-mail.

Officials from both the university and the PR association invited persons to participate on the panel. Panelists represented both Spanish- and English-language media outlets with the majority from Spanish-language outlets.

Marquez notes that the target audience was mainly public relations professionals.

"We find that journalists are generally happy to participate in professional development seminars," says Hampton, "because it helps them to build the relationships with PR professionals who help them do their jobs, in the same way it helps us do our jobs to build relationships with journalists."

Cost for the seminars ranged from $45 for students to $90 for non-HPRA members. UCLA media relations employees attended at no cost. Both the HPRA and UCLA staff utilized e-mail blasts to publicize the seminars.

"Results have been fantastic," Marquez says of the partnership. "We've strengthened our relation-ships with Spanish-language media by having direct access to various Latino media panelists and introduc-ing UCLA public relations professionals to them."

Romina Bongiovanni, president, HPRA (Los Angeles, CA), says: "We appreciate UCLA's partnership for allowing us to focus on what we do best — provide networking and growth opportunities to Hispanic public relations professionals and students — and not having to worry about finding a suitable, affordable place to host our HPRA Professional Development Seminar for two years in a row."

When holding a seminar of this kind, they advise, create a panel that will appeal to your target audience and spark discussion. Research the seminar topics and identify several potential speakers. Then contact an individual you already know within an organization and seek their opinion about who to invite as a panelist.

Sources: Phil Hampton, Assistant Director; Letisia Marquez, Senior Media Relations Officer; Office of Media Relations, UCLA, Los Angeles, CA. Phone (310) 825-2585.
E-mail: phampton@support.ucla.edu or lmarquez@support.ucla.edu
Romina Bongiovanni, President, Hispanic Public Relations Association, Los Angeles, CA.
E-mail: romina.bongiovanni@edelman.com

The Hispanic Public Relations Association (Los Angeles, CA) features professional development seminars made possible through a partnership with UCLA in its member newsletters.

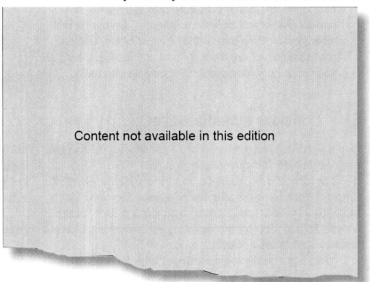

Content not available in this edition

33 Consider Weekend Timing for Press Conferences

Whoever said "never on a Sunday" obviously didn't need to compete with other agencies for local news time.

Depending on the nature of your organization and announcement you are making, consider hosting a press conference on a Saturday morning or early Sunday afternoon.

Often, the weekend news crew is looking for some local features and story ideas to fill what can be a typically slow news day. By "spoon-feeding" them an event, complete with key persons on hand to interview, you just may find your

organization as the lead story for that night's broadcast or an "above-the-fold" article in the next day's paper.

In determining when to host your news conference, keep in mind that a weekend would not be appropriate in cases where reporters may want to do follow-up or sidebar stories in which they would need to solicit input from other agencies, government or other entities normally available during the Monday through Friday work week.

34 'Nosy' Reporters Can Be an Asset

Never underestimate reporters — even in the midst of a crisis, they can be an asset.

Granted, reporters aren't always going to be able to provide you more information on an issue than what you already know. But they are indeed a resource — and sometimes when you least expect it. They can be your source for the rumor mill, and they can help you head off information at the pass. Reporters in the midst of covering a crisis will likely be hunting for information anywhere they can. Talking to them regularly — so long as it's a controlled discussion — will allow communicators to gauge how things are being communicated elsewhere, maybe stop a rumor or gather much-needed information on what is taking place and how your organization is being perceived.

35 Highlight Impressive Facts With a 'Top 10' List

Don't overcomplicate things. Next time you're looking to share interesting facts or reasons to support a specific cause, consider a "Top 10" List.

That technique worked well several years ago for Middle Tennessee State University (MTSU) of Murfreesboro, TN, where officials created a publication highlighting the top 10 facts people might not know about MTSU.

The list pulled key information into one easy-to-read, easy-to-share publication, says F. Douglas Williams, executive director, marketing and communications.

"These facts are well-known strengths of the university," says Williams.

While the Top 10 publication is no longer produced, the list is included in MTSU's visitors guide and also referred to throughout its facts-and-figures guide. The university produces and distributes 5,000 copies of each publication every year.

"When we first developed the Top 10 list publication, we wanted to include facts that people might not be aware of and that gave people a good feel for MTSU," says Williams. "We also included things unique to MTSU, such as signature programs in aerospace, recording industry and the concrete management program."

He and other staff decided to create the list after being inspired by late-night talk show host David Letterman's popular Top 10 list. If your organization already has an extensive facts sheet, he advises pulling the most interesting, newsworthy and/or appealing top 10 and creating and sharing them in list format.

Be sure to keep the information fresh, says Williams, noting that MTSU's 2008 Visitors Guide contains an updated Top 10 list.

"Each year we look at the list and reevaluate it," he says. "The marketing office gets input from other people on campus, most notably the publications and graphics office." The input gathered is informal, he says, and while the list generally remains the same from year to year, updates and changes are made as needed.

Williams says that a list of this kind is appealing to readers because it is easier to remember and repeat than reading this information in a longer narrative format.

Source: F. Douglas. Williams, Executive Director, Marketing and Communications, Middle Tennessee State University, Murfreesboro, TN. Phone (615) 898-2919. E-mail: fdwillia@mtsu.edu

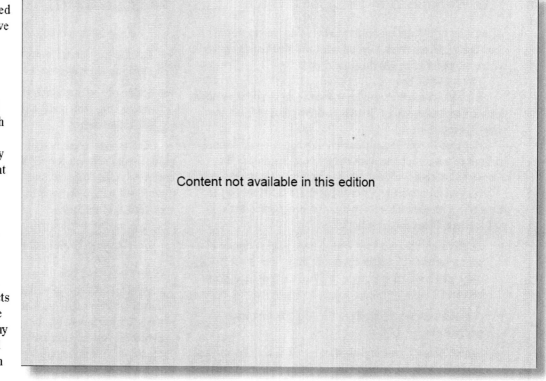

Content not available in this edition

36 Sending Press Releases by Fax or E-mail

While you may still mail news releases when you have a large number of media organizations on your list, chances are you use fax or e-mail methods more often. But don't assume your news release will be read just because you hit send. Take steps to make sure it is not only read, but that it gets into the appropriate hands as well.

When e-mailing, remember that the subject line makes the difference between it being opened or deleted. Be specific and brief. Follow up with a phone call to make sure the news editor, assignment editor or specific reporter received the e-mail and all attachments, and whether it's in an accessible format.

For a news release you send by fax:

- **Use a cover letter.** Print it on letterhead with "FAX transmission" across top in bold, underlined letters. Include the date; number of pages; name and/or title of person you are sending it to; as well as your name, title, organization name and fax, phone and cell numbers; plus a short note describing what is being sent.

- **Name the recipient.** Fax it to the specific reporter who covers that type of news (e.g., education reporter). Don't send it to the general fax number without a specific person's name and/or title.

- **Personalize it.** Include a short note in the cover letter describing what you are sending, e.g., "(Reporter name),

I thought your readers would like to know about our Race for the Cure, Saturday, Aug. 10 at Tree Park. Please call me with any questions (your phone number and cell phone number). Sincerely, (your name, title, and organization name)".

- **Spell it out.** If your release is more than one page, include the word "MORE" at the end of each page. Write "END" at the end of your release to indicate there are no more pages.

37 Add Timeless Stories To Online Press Room

Add evergreen story ideas or complete stories in your online press room. That way, reporters searching your site for story ideas will have a starting point complete with ideas of persons to contact and photos/video to shoot.

For inspiration, check out these online press rooms' "evergreen story" section:

The National Governors Association (www.nga.org/newsroom/evergreen/)

Maryland Office of Tourism (www.mdisfun.org/press_room/evergreen.asp)

The Coordinated Campaign for Learning Disabilities (www.focusonlearning.org/mediaroom.htm) — Scroll to "News You Can Use" section for "timeless" news stories.

38 Working With TV? Think 'B-roll'

When a local TV station sends a crew to do a story about your organization, think beyond who will do the talking and where the reporter might do a stand-up.

Think B-roll, too.

B-roll is video that will be shown as the reporter or news anchor narrates the story. It adds to the story and illustrates what's being said.

Because B-roll doesn't involve anyone having to stand in front of a microphone answering questions, this is the chance to get some of your other important people on screen.

As you escort the reporter to meet the main contact for the story, arm yourself with two or three suggestions for B-roll footage. Ideas might include:

- Staff/volunteers working with clients one on one or in a group setting (if patient confidentiality is an issue, focus only on client's hands, toys or other tools used in your services).

- A construction project, from the construction team's perspective.

- A busy area of your organization, such as a reception desk or children's play area (be sure confidential information is

nowhere in the shot or on a computer screen).

- Behind-the-scenes shots of people preparing food, stocking shelves or other daily maintenance duties.

- Video of the main interview subject for the story interacting with staff, clients or volunteers in a natural-looking manner.

Remember to get both a verbal OK and a signed photo/video media consent for all clients or volunteers who may be onscreen. Also, keep in mind that the TV station may keep this stock footage on hand indefinitely to use whenever your nonprofit is in the news.

39 Worthy of a Press Release

If someone told you it couldn't be done (whatever "it" may be), and you did it, that's newsworthy. Have you solved an especially difficult problem or developed a more efficient way of doing something? Share your achievements and get some recognition for your creativity and ingenuity by issuing a press release.

40 | Hot Sheets: A Versatile Communications Tool

More detailed than a typical fact sheet, a hot sheet can serve as a useful tool when communicating with various community members, from donors to journalists.

"A hot sheet traditionally has been a communication piece that highlights 'hot' news or 'hot button' information — usually in a concise manner," says Larry Anderson, magazine director, DePauw University (Greencastle, IN).

Compiling detailed information in a convenient and concise format is something your organization can incorporate into various aspects of your marketing and outreach efforts. Depending on the type of information you include and the frequency of publication, it may be something your staff can easily produce in-house with little cost. "I write a two-sided 8 1/2 X 14-inch sheet called Briefings in which I include news items, interesting facts, updates and other strategic information that supports the marketing goals and priorities of the university. It's type only (no photos) and inexpensive to print," says Anderson.

One major advantage of a hot sheet is your staff, volunteers and donors can utilize it in different ways to share information about your organization. "The greatest benefit of Briefings is that it brings together in one place the accurate and consistent information we most want to communicate to our key publics. The information I include in Briefings is simply not available in one place anywhere else and division staff members don't have the time to gather it all from separate sources. By compiling the news and information into the simple format of Briefings, I not only provide a useful tool for staff members, but also enlist them into a communication network that more effectively and more widely tells the story we want told about the university."

Source: Larry G. Anderson, Magazine Director, DePauw University, Greencastle, IN. Phone (765) 658-4628. E-mail: landersn@depauw.edu

Content not available in this edition

DePauw University's hot sheets, Briefings, provide media, staff, volunteers and donors a quick glance at campus news, factoids and strategic information.

Additional Hot Sheet Uses

Larry Anderson, magazine director, DePauw University (Greencastle, IN), illustrates how his organization makes use of its Briefings hot sheet:

- Development officers carry it with them to update donors and often leave it behind for alumni and donors to read.

- It's provided to annual fund volunteers not only to keep them informed, but also to provide information for them to include in letters and other communication to their fellow alumni.

- It's given as a handout at alumni events on campus as well as at regional alumni events across the country.

- Annual fund phonathon student callers receive it as a resource for talking with alumni donors.

- The admission office provides a copy to prospective students and their parents. This year, the alumni office printed a hangtag to accompany Briefings and mailed a copy to accepted students to keep them informed about the university.

- The career services center provides Briefings to employers to help demonstrate the kinds of experiences students — potential employees — have at the university.

41 Herald Your Awards

If your organization has received a prestigious honor, be proactive in making the entire community aware of your accomplishment.

"Being named one of the nation's top 100 hospitals was a unique honor that required a unique strategy," says Susan Goschie, director of communications and marketing, Silverton Hospital (Silverton, OR). The hospital was eager to get the word out about its accomplishment and used several methods to ensure the community knew about its award.

Goschie explains the specific steps they took to spread the word:

1. Issued press releases to the four community newspapers that serve the communities in their service area. Since they were one of two hospitals in their category to receive this honor on the West Coast, they also released this information to the regional press.

2. Banners proclaiming this honor were hung in the hospital and in eight associated clinics.

3. Two articles ran in their weekly employee newsletter to congratulate staff on their contribution to attaining the honor.

4. "100 Top" t-shirts were developed for each employee and volunteer.

5. Stickers were ordered and distributed for use on appropriate outgoing correspondence.

6. Signs were placed in high traffic areas of the hospital and related clinics.

7. A signature line was created for their ads.

8. An article was written about the honor for their publication Healthview that is mailed to their service area.

Whatever methods you choose, highlighting the honors you receive is a terrific way to renew the community's interest in your organization and remind them how hard you've been working to serve them. "Consumers sometimes think 'bigger is better.' Receiving this award was a vehicle to remind our public of the quality care they have in their hometown," Goschie says.

Source: Susan Goschie, Director of Communications and Marketing, Silverton Hospital, Silverton, OR.
E-mail: sgoschie@silvhosp.org

42 Maximize Extraordinary Recognition

When your organization receives extraordinary recognition, make the most of it.

That was the challenge put on staff at Chestnut Hill College (Philadelphia, PA) after *Sports Illustrated* ranked it in the "Top 5 Commencement Speakers in the Country."

The May 2007 article, distributed online, was also available via the front page of CNN.com and picked up by many other news outlets on the Web, says Lisa Mixon, media relations manager.

"Chestnut Hill's speaker, Dick Vermeil, was chosen from college and university commencement speakers nationwide to be in the SI article," Mixon explains. The coverage came as a surprise to college officials, since the story was picked up by SI through the ProfNet service to which the college subscribes. The service issues news alerts when the college's name is found on the Internet.

"From the SI story, other newspapers nationwide also picked up the information and included it in stories of their own," she adds.

To inform internal and external audiences of the recognition, Mixon says, "our first priority was to make sure that the entire college was aware of the honor by sending out e-mails to more than 500 people with links to the article so everyone could read it or access it. We also made sure that all other stakeholders of the college (alumni, friends, donors) were told about the honor, through e-mails and phone calls."

Staff also posted hard copies of the SI story on bulletin boards throughout campus.

"It is very important, especially for nonprofits, to make the most of positive recognition and accomplishments because it communicates to your stakeholders and the public that your organization is successful," says Mixon. "It is very important to communicate these achievements throughout your organization, because it creates energy and excitement about what your organization is doing, and that others are recognizing the work that you do. Communicating that recognition to the public also ensures that the community knows about your organization — and that can create new relationships through these achievements."

Source: Lisa Mixon, Media Relations Manager, Chestnut Hill College, Philadelphia, PA. Phone (215) 753-3664.
E-mail: mixonl@chc.edu

43 Media Wisdom

In Errol Morris' film "Fog of War," former Secretary of Defense Robert McNamara said, "Never answer the question that is asked. Answer the question you wish were asked." To shape others' perception of you — the essence of good media — train yourself to speak only what you want others to hear.

44 Dedicate Your Summer to a Media Campaign

Spring 2006 brought excitement and challenges for Sarah Ward, director of university relations, and Meredith Long, sports information director, Chowan University (Murfreesboro, NC). The school changed its status from college to university and its mascot — two big events happening at the same time.

Ward and Long used the timing to their advantage and utilized the summer months to start "Summer Buzz," a local, regional and national media campaign promoting the changes. Below are key actions taken to promote the campaign:

1. Ward and Long met with the university president to get a general direction of how the media campaign should go. They set specific goals to get the university's name out and a timeline for those goals. The president also gave them a budget.
2. A media packet was put together, which contained official press releases, contact information and disks with pictures, graphics of the new logo and head shots of university leaders.
3. Since Murfreesboro is in a rural part of the state, a major objective was to make as many regional media contacts as possible. Every media outlet in the area, plus some nationally, received the packet. Contacts were made with newspapers, radio and TV stations to set up face-to-face meetings.
4. Ten meetings were set up during the summer. They met with editors, news directors, sports departments and secretaries — anyone who was willing to meet. They also brought along promotional items to leave with the news departments or other staff at the outlets.
5. Ten billboards were put up along main highways in eastern North Carolina promoting the name changes.

The effort was successful because not only did the university's name get printed in places it wouldn't have prior to "Summer Buzz," but the new contacts and names they received were priceless.

Source: Sarah Ward, Director of University Relations, and Meredith Long, Sports Information Director, Chowan University, Murfreesboro, NC. Phone (252) 398-6319. E-mail: wards@chowan.edu

Set Media Campaign Goals, Deadlines

Because the "Summer Buzz" campaign had multiple components, Chowan University's Ward and Long made sure they stayed on track to get everything done by fall. The following guide outlined each goal and its estimated and actual completion dates:

- Goal: Promote recent changes and university celebration in the community and with media contacts and university friends.
  By: September 2006
  Completed: Sept. 7

- Goal: Establish face-to-face contacts with local and regional media contacts.
  By: September 2006
  Completed: Sept. 7

- Goal: Update media kit (hard copies and on CD) for media contacts.
  By: May 2006
  Completed: May 6

- Goal: Continue media relationships through visits, e-mail and phone calls.
  By: May 2007
  Completed: in progress

45 Work to Improve Your Media Relations Skills

Building media relationships and developing solid media relations skills will benefit your communications efforts in the long term.

James O'Connor, associate director for public relations, University of Northern Iowa (Cedar Falls, IA), shares tips on creating and maintaining positive media relationships:

1. Meet with the media. Ask them what you are doing right and wrong so you can improve your approach.
2. Understand the media's needs. Find out if they have an editorial calendar so you can release timely stories.
3. Make the media aware of your experts.
4. Prepare your staff. Offer staff a tip sheet so they know how to handle a media call.
5. Role-play media calls. Have someone ask you questions and practice your responses out loud.
6. Establish relationships with the media. Don't wait for a bad situation to create those relationships.
7. Reach out to various mediums (e.g., radio, trade associations, etc.).
8. Don't overuse news releases. Call the media with a tip if the idea doesn't warrant its own release.

Source: James O'Connor, Associate Director for Public Relations, Office of University Marketing and Public Relations, University of Northern Iowa, Cedar Falls, IA.

46   Provide Staff With Tools They Need to Handle Media Encounters With Finesse

Don't wait until the reporter shows up at your co-worker's door to offer media relations advice. Ensuring all staff members are well-versed in basic media relations strategies will increase your organization's chances of receiving news coverage.

"We felt it was important to offer faculty some suggestions before they were contacted by the media and not after," says Bob Skipper, media relations director, university relations, Western Kentucky University (Bowling Green, KY). "We do not try to centrally control access to faculty by reporters, although we do offer ourselves as resources if needed. We wanted faculty to feel comfortable talking to reporters and to not ignore requests for interviews, thereby missing an opportunity for publicity."

Skipper created the guidelines (shown at right) roughly five years ago.

"I developed the content, pulling some of the information from my colleagues at other universities and some from my experience as a newspaper reporter," he says. "Some information came from other websites and much of it came during face-to-face conversations and presentations at conferences."

Faculty members were made aware of the document through mass e-mails.

With the in-house resource, "our faculty now seems more comfortable with talking with reporters, and many of the reporters we work with know which faculty members deliver the better interviews," says Skipper. "We have been working on presentations that we plan to start making at faculty departmental meetings at least once a year and this information will be included."

Skipper shares some advice for other nonprofit communicators who are considering creating this type of document, saying "Look around the Web for information that can be adapted to your situation. Also, if you have a relationship already developed with local reporters, ask for their input. They can better tell you what they find helpful and a hindrance."

Source: Bob Skipper, Media Relations Director, University Relations, Western Kentucky University, Bowling Green, KY. Phone (270) 745-4295. E-mail: bob.skipper@wku.edu

Guidelines Help Staff Deal With Media

Interested in creating a handy tip sheet on working with the news media? Share it with your co-workers, board members and volunteers, and possibly post online so this important information is always just a mouse click away.

For inspiration, look to the "Working With the Media" publication that staff at Western Kentucky University (Bowling Green, KY) can refer to when dealing with reporters and other media representatives.

The staff and other key players who may need to represent the university in the press can feel confident doing so, thanks to the guidelines, below, developed for them by Bob Skipper, media relations director.

Working With the Media

We rely on the news media to get the Western story to the public, but they can only accurately report on what's going on if they get accurate information. Here are some simple guidelines for dealing with a call from a reporter:

- Obtain the reporter's name and affiliation and ask exactly how you can be of assistance.

- Once you know what the reporter needs, determine if you are the appropriate spokesperson. If not, refer the reporter to the correct person or to the media relations office at 745-4295.

- If possible, schedule a face-to-face interview, especially if the material is complex. This will give you a chance to better explain the subject and provide supporting material. Be flexible; distance and deadlines often make this impossible.

- If you need time to gather the facts, or to collect your thoughts, ask for it. Ask the reporter to call back in a few minutes.

- Be ready to give your message. Prepare a single communications objective and two or three secondary points you want to make.

- Remember, don't say anything you don't want to see in print or on the news. Since conflict is news, reporters often ask questions to bring out the conflict in stories. State your position in positive terms and try not to fan controversy.

- Anticipate tough questions. If you'd like help preparing, give the media relations office a call. If you'd rather not answer a question, say so. If you don't know the answer, say so. But be willing to direct the reporter to someone who can answer the question.

- Use simple language and speak in short sentences.

- Be concise. Reporters work with a limited amount of time and/or space, so get to the point.

- Respect deadlines by returning calls promptly.

- Don't expect a reporter to show you the story before it is published; it conflicts with journalistic ethics. If you fear a point has not been understood, ask the reporter to repeat it. Let the reporter know how to get in touch with you if there are further questions.

47 All-electronic Media Kit Commemorates Anniversary

If your organization is celebrating a significant anniversary or milestone, how about creating a commemorative media kit that not only informs the news media about the event, but educates your supporters and the community as well?

Consider going all-electronic to keep costs at a minimum while capitalizing on the latest computer technology to share the timely information.

Staff with Clarkson College (Omaha, NE) created an all-electronic media kit to commemorate its 120th anniversary in 2008.

"We decided to create a media kit for the 120th anniversary to create a greater awareness of the activities included in our celebration," says Melodae Morris, senior director of marketing and public relations. "The goal is to capitalize on another branding opportunity to create a memorable impression in the community with prospective students, parents and alumni."

The kit was created in less than a week using several staple public relations pieces, including a backgrounder, historical timeline and fact sheet, along with a media release

and photos, says Kelsey Archer, assistant director of marketing and public relations.

While much of the timeline was already intact, there was some information missing. Morris says the additional information was found in the college's historical archive and in the history book, Learning to Care, which covers the first century of the college's history. Plus, staff searched through boxes of memorabilia, scrapbooks and photos.

They posted the media kit on the university's website and e-mailed it to media contacts. The only cost involved was that of the staff time needed to create and distribute these materials.

"The response has been exceedingly favorable," says Morris. "The materials are achieving what we hoped. We are attracting new alumni membership every day and so far, the media coverage has been great."

Sources: Kelsey Archer, Assistant Director of Marketing and Public Relations; Melodae Morris, Senior Director of Marketing and Public Relations, Clarkson College, Omaha, NE.
Phone (402) 552-6209 (Archer) or (402) 552-6114 (Morris).

48 PR Media Mistakes to Avoid

Refine your media relations plan in light of this list of "what to do and not do:"

1. **Poor timing.** Do consider lead time for television news, radio, daily and weekly newspapers and other media. Don't call a radio station five minutes before the top-of-the-hour news broadcast with a story idea. Don't call a TV station's assignment editor at 3 p.m. for the day's story. Don't send a story to a weekly newspaper that misses the deadline for that week's publication and will be out of date for the next one.

2. **Poorly written news releases.** Do grab the reader quickly. Do follow up with information about the event or activity. Do keep it concise while covering pertinent details and contact information. Don't use insider jargon that isn't part of mainstream conversation; doing so won't impress editors who have little time to read all the press releases that pop up in their e-mail. Do write in plain and simple language.

3. **Put-downs of your competition.** Don't gossip about your competitors or point fingers, even if it's just a sideways verbal comment as you walk with a reporter to an interview subject's office; news reporters will ultimately let them know and develop a poor regard for you.

4. **Too much hype.** Don't overplay an event just to get news attention, as that will only harm your credibility.

5. **Too many new releases.** Don't send a news release for every minor development unless you want to teach news directors and editors to tune out your correspondence and distrust your news judgment.

6. **Overuse of formal news releases and quotes.** Don't overwrite. Do sometimes send a simple e-mail "pitch" sheet that suggests a story and lists contact information.

7. **Failing to get your name in the lead.** Don't make readers wade through three paragraphs to find a tie to your organization. Do work your name into the headline, lead sentence and photo cutlines.

49 Rule of Thumb

Choosing the Right Media — Selecting the right media for your message can be challenging, but keep this in mind: The more important the message, the more personally it should be delivered.

Putting a human presence with a message through direct interaction dramatically increases its impact. On the other hand, blanketing a wide audience with a general advertisement relies on sheer number of viewers or listeners.

50 Stay on Topic When Facing Overly Aggressive Media

When you are in a live interview situation, whether on the radio or at a press conference, staying on message is important, especially when dealing with confrontational media representatives.

When faced with an unyielding media contact, you can take steps to make sure your message is heard.

Rosalee Rush, director of communications, Bloomsburg University of Pennsylvania (Bloomsburg, PA), shares an example of how she handled a situation at a previous job position in Michigan:

"I was in a press conference where the state and local organizations were announcing the creation of 1,200 new jobs in a local community. Earlier that morning we learned that another major company had just announced the layoff of more than 5,000 employees. Reporters asked what the state intended to do about the layoff and how it was going to impact the local community. Many of the questions were centered on the layoffs, instead of the current topic.

"Our response was: 'We are saddened to hear about the recent announcement by X company; however, we are glad for the creation of today's jobs as this will help offset some

of the job losses and economic impact. These 1,200 jobs are estimated to contribute $X dollars in direct spending to the community.'"

Responding in a way that tied the overall message to the response helped to deflect some of the negative attention and stay on message.

Rush offers these tips for staying on topic in such a situation:

- Listen for any opportunity to steer the conversation back to the current announcement or topic.

- Repeat their question and relate it to your topic. Relay that you understand the question and explain how it relates to this particular situation.

- Other options include simply stating that those questions or concerns will be addressed at a later time; at this time you will answer only questions relating to this particular topic.

Source: Rosalee Rush, Director of Communications, Bloomsburg University of Pennsylvania, Bloomsburg, PA. Phone (570) 489-4043.

51 Show Grace Under Pressure During a Crisis

Charitable organizations of all types and sizes may one day find themselves in the midst of an unfortunate incident or full-blown crisis attracting public and media attention. And suddenly, you're in charge as the spokesperson.

How you conduct yourself during a crisis can have a lasting effect in the public's mind.

Develop a media crisis strategy long before the occasion arises.

During the crisis —

- **Don't cave in to unexpected pressure.** This is not the time to make a quick exit or improvise answers. Listen to media questions, then tell reporters you need a brief time to assess the situation and gather facts. Assure them you will strive to have information by deadline. Then do so.

- **Deal with questions immediately at hand.** Don't offer more facts that inadvertently could fuel a fire.

- **Ask the highest authority to define your role.** Your CEO may elect to take over as spokesperson.

- **Assemble all staff with knowledge of the situation.** Brainstorm to develop a solution and ways to prevent repeating mistakes. Be prepared to offer positive steps at the same time you reveal the bad news.

After the damage has occurred —

- **Identify your most articulate and respected supporter to give updates to the media** or tell why they stand

behind your organization despite its trials.

- **Continue business as usual if appropriate.** If an event closely follows a public relations disaster, view it as an opportunity to show strength despite adversity.

- **Thank reporters who have been objective or supportive.**

Displaying grace under pressure following a crisis may even attract an entirely new base of support from people who paid little attention to you before.

---

52 Which Media Investments Offer Biggest Payback?

 "What are the biggest challenges that are facing nonprofit communicators today?"

"The biggest challenge is understanding which investments in new media really pay off and which ones do not; these are critical budget and staffing issues. In lean times, this is especially problematic. Conventional wisdom about Internet use may not be the reality and it seems that each target market has a different set of media behaviors. One thing is for sure, traditional public relations practices no longer pay off as they once did."

— Larry D. Lauer, Vice Chancellor for Marketing and Communication, Texas Christian University (Fort Worth, TX)

53 Create Notable Press Releases

Dozens of press releases cross a reporter's desk daily. How can you ensure your news gets attention?

The news release is an underestimated tool for engaging a reporter and their audience, says Susan Harrow, media trainer, marketing strategist and CEO, prsecrets.com (Oakland, CA). A common mistake made by organizations, Harrow says, is to pitch its services, not story topics and ideas.

Here are ways to effectively offer your organization's stories through press releases:

- **Use a strong headline.** Here's a winning example of one of Harrow's headlines: "While most kindergarteners are picking their noses and feeding their broccoli to the dog, six-year-old Jace Richards was finishing his first book."

- **Back up the headline with statistics and sources.** Using stats saves a reporter time, gives your story validity and brings them directly to the best sources, including your organization. For example, here's the first paragraph of the Jace Richards press release: "Last month, more than 60,000 grownups attempted to write a novel by participating in National Novel Writing Month and nearly 90 percent of them failed. Depressing? Sure. Especially when you consider kids across the country are taking time out between Power Rangers and well, time-outs, to write bestsellers."

- **Tie your story into a trend.** "Journalists are always looking for the latest trend," Harrow says. The press release successfully brings attention to the trend of best-selling children's authors: "These young scribes, with their uninhibited passion and unfiltered emotions, are turning out profound and meaningful books that speak to adults and kids."

- **Be specific.** Keep specifics in your press release. Note the specifics and statistics in the following paragraph: "Kindergarten student Jace Richards was inspired to write a book about what it's like to live with an autistic brother. His book, My Brother's Keeper: A Kindergartener's View of Autism, is striking a chord with the rapidly growing number of families affected by autism, as well as students and educators who are looking for ways to understand the increasing number of autistic children entering the public school system annually — autism affects approximately one in 166 children. School systems have been buying copies by the thousands for distribution in classrooms."

- **Don't be too promotional.** Think about what you can do for the reporter's audience. The child author story makes an interesting story and offers news on an available best-selling book.

- **Don't be boring.** Offer statistics and information that's startling, unusual or provocative, but be sure to back up what you're saying, Harrow says.

- **Provide contacts and sources.** End press releases with contacts for press materials and interviews.

Source: Susan Harrow, CEO, prsecrets.com, Oakland, CA. Phone (888) 839-4190. E-mail: susanh@prsecrets.com

54 Create a Media Policy That Benefits Organization, Media

Baptist Memorial Health Care Corporation (Memphis, TN) maintains a media relations policy that has proven mutually rewarding.

"The biggest advantage (of the policy) is that it helps ensure reporters get the information they need to make their stories informative for their audiences," says Ayoka Pond, public relations manager. "The policy also helps make our spokespeople more confident and comfortable with communicating with the media."

Baptist's five-part policy requires all media inquiries go through the public relations department. No exceptions. Additionally, a public relations representative must accompany the media while on campus and be present during interviews and photo shoots, regardless if these are with a patient, physician or Baptist employee.

"One of the main reasons for this policy is because we can quickly put reporters in touch with the best expert for their story," Pond says. "Another reason for our policy is because many of our colleagues don't fully understand how the media work. Some are fearful of reporters; others don't understand reporters' deadlines and processes. We're a liaison between reporters and our colleagues. We also find that our patients are very appreciative of our support before and during a media interview."

To make a media relations policy like this work, Pond says the nonprofit must utilize it consistently and offer no exceptions. Additionally, the organization needs to consider media requests a priority.

"Requests for interviews take priority over everything else we do, so if a reporter calls us, we immediately stop what we're doing to work on that request," she says.

When a request comes in, Pond and her staff track down background information for both the reporter and the spokesperson. They also work with the spokesperson to ensure they are prepared for the interview, says Pond, noting, "Reporters really appreciate that and come to us for health care interviews because we respect and understand their deadlines."

Source: Ayoka Pond, Public Relations Manager, Baptist Memorial Health Care Corporation, Baptist Corporate Communications, Memphis, TN. Phone (901) 227-3503. E-mail: ayoka.pond@bmhcc.org

55 Become a Top-notch Interviewee

So you've agreed to an interview with the media. Now what?

Preparing ahead of time and keeping some media-specific pointers in mind will lead to a more successful interview.

"For any medium, think about what you want to say in advance and write down key points," advises Teresa Mannix, director of news and public information, University of Mary Washington (Fredricksburg, VA). Keep these key points in front of you for a radio interview, and if you are relaying technical or statistical information, feel free to have them on hand for a television interview, she says.

"Anticipate questions and prepare answers for them," Mannix says. "In addition, be prepared to transition possible negative questions into ways to communicate your key points."

For example, take the initiative to refocus an interview by responding to an interviewer's question or comment with: "That's an interesting point, but our main focus is (fill in the blank)."

Mannix shares pointers specific to interviews for television, radio or print venues:

- **For TV interviews:** "Make sure the visuals are there, e.g., know what is in the background; make sure you are wearing a color that will show up well on camera; bring visual aids to illustrate your points. When doing a TV interview, have a conversation with the reporter and not the camera. It will help calm your nerves and it will look better on air. If you are sitting, make sure you are sitting with good posture and that you are not nervously swiveling in a chair or clicking a pen, etc."

- **For radio interviews:** "Make sure you are in a quiet location (if conducting the interview over the phone). If you have any audio that illustrates your points, share that with the reporter."

- **For print reporters:** "It is easy to say that you will research something you don't know and call them back. Remember that you also have that option with radio and television. Don't try to make something up just to have an on-the-spot answer. And don't speculate as to what may or may not be happening. Just stick to your talking points and the known facts."

Regardless of the medium, Mannix says to also remember to practice ahead of time to avoid "ums"; make sure your cell phone is off and that you are not chewing gum.

Finally, she says, realize that, like many other tasks, developing solid interviewing skills takes practice, so view each interview as an opportunity to hone your skills.

Source: Teresa Mannix, Director of News and Public Information, University of Mary Washington, Fredericksburg, VA. Phone (540) 654-1055. E-mail: tmannix@umw.edu

56 Communicate Bad News Without Placing Blame

When sharing "bad news" with the community, it pays to be proactive and reach out to the media before they contact you. It is also crucial that your organization resists the urge to point fingers.

"We've had a couple of instances when we have received potentially contaminated purchased or donated food," says Jack Parris, public relations manager, Community Food Bank (Tucson, AZ). "One was contaminated hamburger meat and one was the recent tomato salmonella concern. In both cases, we immediately sent out a local press release to the media explaining our position and, in the case of the meat, what we had done to resolve the matter. In the case of the potential to-mato problem, we received assurances from the growers that they knew their product was not contaminated and passed along that information."

Parris and his co-workers sent out press releases addressing both situations before they were contacted by the media. The food bank received local TV and print coverage regarding both issues.

When sharing what could be perceived as bad news, state the facts without blame, he says. "We do not place blame, but explain the situation, put forth the steps we have made to resolve the problem and reassure our clients that we have their best interest in mind."

Conveying necessary information without placing blame will allow you to inform the community and the media without adding unneeded drama to the situation. Ideally, it will also avoid any negative press about your organization.

Parris offers these tips for communicating negative news effectively:

- Keep your language straightforward, factual but not alarming.

- Let the community know that you recognize the problem and will take steps to resolve it.

- Don't panic and don't volunteer information.

- Consider every conversation as being on the record.

- Never say "no comment."

Source: Jack Parris, Public Relations Manager, Community Food Bank, Tucson, AZ. Phone (520) 622-0525. E-mail: JParris@communityfoodbank.org

57 Eight Ways to Get in the News

1. **Pick up on trends.** Seeing more teens donating to your shelter? More volunteers e-mailing digital photos? More online volunteering? Being on the cutting edge of a trend is news.

2. **Turn stats into faces.** Your food drive brought in 10,000 pounds of nonperishables? Great! Now tell about the people who collected food and the families it will feed. With recipients' okay, invite a news crew to come along as you distribute food.

3. **Give experts a voice.** What needs does your nonprofit meet? Social? Spiritual? Lifesaving? Think of the people who provide that service — or who train others to do so — and ways they can share this expertise.

4. **Think contrasts.** A grandmother/grandson volunteer team; a janitor who gives $50,000; a five-star chef who volunteers at a soup kitchen; normally apathetic teens cheerfully fitting new shoes on the feet of needy children all make great stories.

5. **Look beyond local news sections.** Pitch a story to the sports department about the key staff/board member in his third decade as a referee. Tell the food editor about the volunteer who uses apples from her tree and her grandmother's recipe to make snacks for children at your daycare center.

6. **Feed them tidbits of filet mignon, not buckets of bologna.** As much as you'd like to be in the news every day, think quality over quantity. Pitch 12 to 26 stories a year with high impact, not 52 with mediocre appeal.

7. **Get in bed with an unusual partner.** What persons, business or "rival" nonprofit would you least expect to support you? Call them. The motorcycle club giving to the pediatric unit or sports adversaries teaming up for a worthy cause makes great press.

8. **Give them a "Top 10" list.** Identify an area of need your agency can address — preferably with a "news hook" — and share your 10 best tips (e.g., keeping children safe during summer break, interacting with a newly widowed person, planting a garden to attract songbirds).

58 Media Database: Valuable Communications Tool

Finding a versatile media database will streamline your media outreach and save your organization valuable time.

"A media database helps nonprofits save time, money and staff resources while trying to promote and create awareness about the organization. An organization should know the reporters who cover their efforts or subject area. That way, you know where to go when you need something published or want to create awareness about your campaign," says James Martinez, media relations specialist, National PTA (Chicago, IL).

The National PTA uses Cision (formerly known as Bacons) for its media monitoring and media database. The database allows organizations to search contacts by name, publication, beat, top 100 publications by circulation or a combination of features. The National PTA uses various search options depending on the nature of the story and the type of publication they are targeting.

"If the campaign we're working on is more focused (e.g., education policy), we'll send the news release via e-mail to education reporters. If the topic is more general (e.g., school violence), we might consider sending something on wire so that as many news outlets, editors and even bloggers can pick it up," says Martinez.

Deciding on the best method to contact reporters can be difficult. Some may prefer e-mail while others prefer phone inquiries. A media database can provide you with the information you need to find the right contact and approach them in the preferred manor.

Martinez recently used the database to find a reporter who wrote a story the PTA felt was one-sided. They wanted to contact this reporter to discuss the article but could not find any contact information listed in the publication. They found the information within the media database in a matter of seconds.

Cost of the media database software, $3,700 annually.

Source: James Martinez, Media Relations Specialist, National PTA, Chicago, IL. Phone (312) 670-6782, ext. 325.
E-mail: jmartinez@pta.org

59 Help Your Employees Overcome 'Media Suspicion'

Are your organization's employees suspicious of the media — afraid reporters are just out to find something negative they can report?

Take steps to help your colleagues diminish their media reluctance. Point out positive stories the media would jump at the chance to publish. Consider offering an in-house workshop on "Dealing With the Media 101," complete with role-playing and mock interviews using video cameras. Do all you can to help your employees become news advocates for your organization and to deal with the media in an open manner.

60 Take Step Back With Media for Better Outcome

If you find yourself involved in every aspect of orchestrating stories for the media, consider taking a step back for a change.

Doing so may just result in a better story, says Colleen Brinkmann, chief marketing officer, North Texas Food Bank (Dallas, TX). "When the media comes, I introduce them to the right people (staff, donors, volunteers, community partners) and let them do their work. They like that and come back to cover our stories time and time again."

The approach is successful for two reasons, she says:

1. **Transparency** — By not trying to script or control stories, Brinkmann says, "you show the media you have nothing to hide. This is important in conveying your message to prospective donors."

2. **"Outside the box" thinking** — "We think we know what's right because we're 'inside' (an organization). The opinion of someone 'outside' matters too. They may approach it in a way you'd never consider, but it works better for a general audience."

Source: Colleen Townsley Brinkmann, Chief Marketing Officer, North Texas Food Bank, Dallas, TX. Phone (214) 347-9594. E-mail: colleen@ntfb.org

61 When Reporters Want to 'Ask the Expert,' Make Sure It's You

A surefire way to keep your organization top of mind is to keep it in the news. One way to do so is to position yourself with the media as an expert. To make that happen:

- **Determine who from within your organization qualifies as an expert and on what topic(s).** A university president could comment on the college loan crisis, while an academic adviser from the same institution could address employment trends in a certain field. Create a reference list with all names and areas of expertise.

- **Let local news organizations know who they can call.** Circulate your list of experts to local news media and make it easily accessible in your online media center.

- **Be proactive.** When news happens locally, nationally or internationally that your experts could address, be the first to reach out to local media. Say: "I'm calling from XYZ Organization and thought you might be interested in a local slant on the recent news about unemployment."

Taking these steps gets your organization's name out there without the story always being about you while making the reporter's job easier, leading to better relationships.

62 Don't Sever Ties Because of Negative Publicity

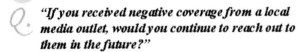

"If you received negative coverage from a local media outlet, would you continue to reach out to them in the future?"

"I would absolutely continue to reach out to the media outlet. It is important to remember that each reporter is simply doing their job. By continuing to reach out to the media outlet, you have the opportunity to build a stronger relationship with them. A better relationship might mean that they would call you to ask about a potentially negative story before it hits the press. This gives you the chance to check their facts, explain the situation from your organization's point of view and practice damage control if needed.

"The worst thing a communications professional can do is ignore a media outlet that ran negative coverage — it allows the media outlet and the public to form negative opinions about you if the only story they've ever heard about you was negative. By staying in contact with the media outlet and forming a good rapport, you can work on promoting the positive things your organization has accomplished and draw attention to the positive instead of the negative."

— Helyse Sina, Public Relations Officer,
Food Bank of Northern Nevada (McCarran, NV)

"I would absolutely continue reaching out to them. Coming from a news background, I understand how many different people touch a story before going to air/print and how easy it is for misinformation to be passed along once you're up against a deadline. But that does not necessarily mean there's a bias against you or your organization.

"If you have received bad coverage, the first thing you need to ask yourself is: Is it true? If so, it's unfair to shift the blame to the media outlet. If it is not true, you need to first work backwards, and review where they got their bad information and why they didn't check with you before going to air/print. Then, work forward, by meeting with the reporter and editorial staff, in person if possible, and explaining what was wrong with the piece. Ask what they can do to fix the problem, and come prepared with ideas of how you can help correct the story. Be transparent, and don't take it personally.

"Also, make sure they know they can call you at any time to fact check a story in the future."

— Sarah Clark, Director of Publications and Media Relations,
Wheaton College (Wheaton, IL)

63 Online Pressroom Dos and Don'ts

Creating an online pressroom can be a great asset to your organization, if it's done correctly. Providing the right kind of information and making it user friendly for media contacts researching your organization is essential.

Ellen Davis, senior director of strategic communications, National Retail Federation (Washington, DC), shares her thoughts on the dos and don'ts for online pressrooms:

DO —

1. **Make as much information available as possible.** Reporters love raw research data and trend information. If you give them information up front, your phone will ring less with information requests.

2. **Ensure contact information is very easy to find.** Include cell phone information if applicable. Try not to send reporters to a general phone number or e-mail address because those are not always monitored frequently.

3. **Keep your website up to date.** There is nothing worse than a press release from 2003 hanging around on your site.

4. **Include information about spokespeople** — their bio and a link to download a high-resolution image.

DON'T —

1. **List the contact information for your CEO or other executives** unless you're okay with reporters going straight to them.

2. **Get too crazy with graphics and design.** Links should be clear and easy to find.

3. **Forget to spell check!** There is nothing worse than a press website with misspelled words.

4. **Require reporters to "register" before getting information.** They will most likely be turned off and not use you as a resource.

Source: Ellen Davis, Senior Director, Strategic Communications, National Retail Federation, Washington, DC. Phone (202) 783-7971. E-mail: davise@nrf.com

64 Create Events That Tantalize the Media

It's possible to make an annual event appeal to the media and the public every year.

Susan Harrow, media trainer, marketing strategist and CEO, prsecrets.com (Oakland, CA), offers the following tips for appealing to the media and ensuring the event's success:

- **Use visuals.** For starters, use visuals to attract attention, says Harrow. When sending a press release about an annual event, include visual information — a cute photo or a close up of a featured product. The photo needs to represent what the event is about, Harrow says.

- **Think small.** Zero in on some aspect of the event — not a large table of items for an auction or a row of works for an art show.

- **Offer fun.** Remember to include a "fun factor." When you invite a reporter to an event, make sure they come when there's excitement. Establish key points at the event for a reporter to cover.

- **Make it interactive.** Offer hands-on activities.

- **Offer prizes.** Giveaways can attract attention. Include gift baskets with key information about your event and organization for guests and the media.

- **Involve a celebrity.** Having a well-known local or national person attend the event generates excitement.

- **Offer a spokesperson.** Make a leader from your organization available to the media to relay what the event

is about, who it benefits and other important information.

- **Be specific.** Always include the precise purpose of your annual event in your press materials. Are you looking for volunteers, money or support? Don't leave anyone guessing.

- **Check for conflicts.** Make sure there's not another big event happening in your area on your event date.

Source: Susan Harrow, CEO, prsecrets.com, Oakland, CA. Phone (888) 839-4190. E-mail: susanh@prsecrets.com

65 Be Ready for TV Interviews

Keep these tips in mind so you're always ready for an on-camera interview:

- Dress appropriately (if you have casual days, keep a suit jacket, shirt and tie or blouse on hand);

- Project energy and enthusiasm with your voice and body language;

- Look at the interviewer, not the camera;

- Choose an uncluttered background. Consider a location with your logo or simple signage so viewers know immediately who you represent.

66 Consider Media Coaching

Having the confidence to answer any media question is just one reason to consider one-on-one media coaching, says Diane DiResta, president, DiResta Communications (New York, NY) and author of *Knockout Presentations: How to Deliver Your Message With Power, Punch and Pizzazz.*

DiResta answers questions about the coaching method for persons who interact with the media:

What are the benefits of one-on-one media coaching?

"Faster results, learning that is focused and tailored to your specific objectives, more successful interviews, greater sales of your products and services, greater brand name recognition, stronger trust and credibility conveyed to the audience."

How often should media coaching be done?

"Start with a one-day or half-day training to learn the basics. To make sure you are at the top of your game, get media coaching before a major or national media interview and when you're offering new message points or a new topic... If you've done a good job of developing message points,

you should be able to do several interviews without being coached each time."

How should you prepare beforehand?

To make the best use of your and your trainer's time, she says, prepare questions in advance, know your target audience and top 10 media outlets, she says. "With a media trainer, you'll be able to develop specific message points targeted to your ideal audience or buyer... (A coaching session should cover) types of media, target audience, image and dress, message points, timing, speaking in sound bites, building relationships with media, answering questions, keeping control of the interview. You should be videotaped even if doing phone interviews. A good coach will teach you how to analyze your performance."

After a major interview, she says, schedule a session with the coach to critique your performance and make adjustments for the next interview.

Source: Diane DiResta, President, DiResta Communications, Inc., New York, NY. E-mail: info@diresta.com

67 Should You Hold a Press Conference?

A press conference, used properly, can be a powerful venue at which to announce exciting developments within your organization. Reserve this communications tool for truly major news, or risk disinterest on the part of the media.

Stephen Burgay, vice president of marketing and communications, Boston University (Boston, MA), says press conferences are most effective when you have significant news with a broad appeal. For example, "introducing a new president or announcing a major grant or celebrating the fact that one of your personnel just received a significant award are all cases worthy of a press conference," he says. "Breaking ground on a major new facility that is going to have an impact on the surrounding community or releasing survey results on some topic of acute interest to the public are other examples."

Creative alternatives to press conferences may suit the situation perfectly. Burgay says in some cases it may be more beneficial to take reporters into the field to showcase your programs at work and humanize your story.

If you decide to hold a press conference, include eye-catching visuals to accompany your announcement.

Burgay says asking these questions can help decide if a press conference is warranted and appropriate:

- Is the news really big?

- Will an editor view your story as front-page/top news material? You are asking newspersons to commit part of their precious news space to you; make it worth their while.

- Does a press conference tell your story in its best light, or would another way, such as a personal tour or one-on-one interview be better?

- Have you chosen a time for your press conference that will increase the chances of the press attending, either on a slow news day or early enough to make the noon or evening news, and made sure it does not conflict with a city council or other regularly covered meeting?

Source: Stephen Burgay, Vice President of Marketing and Communications, Boston University, Boston, MA. E-mail: burgay@bu.edu

68 Press Conference Tip

- One way to get members of the media to attend your press conference is to allow one-on-one time with key representatives associated with your organization. Set up personal interviews with the president or CEO following the press conference. Doing so not only demonstrates your commitment to the press, but also builds goodwill between your organization and media outlets.

69 Highlight Press Releases With a Media Blog

Create a media relations blog to spotlight press releases and include interactive features.

In September 2007, the media relations team at Lourdes College (Sylvania, OH) launched a media relations blog specifically to post press releases. Written by staff, students and alumni, the blog's goal is to communicate the most current Lourdes news to the public, says Heather Hoffman, media coordinator and chief author of the blog.

"Media has become so interactive that I just don't think the typical press release, all text and no action, packs the same pizzazz that an interactive tool like a blog has," says Hoffman. While they still post press releases in an online newsroom, "I enjoy using the blog to post press releases because it allows others to give feedback and comment on stories. It also offers features that typical attachments do not,"

such as the ability to embed videos, slideshows and photos.

The college's Web content administrator and the director of college relations, in conjunction with Thread Information Design (Maumee, OH), created the blog center that includes the media relations blog and others related to the college.

Response from staff, students, alumni and the community has been positive, says Hoffman, noting that the local media has noticed the releases listed on the blog as well.

For nonprofits considering a media blog, Hoffman offers this advice: "Be as interactive as possible. Post videos, photos and allow for dialogue. This will give your reporting an added touch that a typical press release falls short of. Don't be afraid to make your media a dynamic experience!"

Source: Heather Hoffman, Media Coordinator, Lourdes College, Sylvania, OH. Phone (419) 824-3952.

70 Help Media Spread the Good Word

Nonprofits need to learn the skills to get the word out about their good news.

This is difficult for nonprofits for several reasons, including that it's hard for most to see outside themselves, says Ann Higgins, president, Utopia Media Enhancement Services (Red Bank, NJ).

"Often their primary job of developing and implementing program content and the scramble for supporters gobbles up their energy and the ability to realize and market the great stories they have to offer," Higgins says. "Secondly, they lack the day-to-day working knowledge on how to distribute and structure their story and time it to the wandering and frenetic press needs.

"The flip side is the media desperately needs more consumer-friendly content about people and organizations working to make the world a better and safer place."

What can nonprofits do to meet these media needs?

"First, nonprofits need to step back, take a deep breath and understand the business they are in with a plan that stresses their publicity goal, but in a way that makes their daily life easier," Higgins says.

"Getting media attention that sells your message and philosophy is like going to the gym. If it's not easy to get to and you have no plan for realistic day-to-day success, you will only be feeling guilty at day's end."

Working with a media coach often provides solutions for nonprofits lacking expertise in this area. Media consulting firms can help nonprofits learn to see great stories and opportunities, develop ongoing media relationships and build strong media contacts.

"Great ideas and stories should bubble from the bottom of your organization to the top," Higgins says. "The people, the work you do and the results you get need to be fashioned in a display method that highlights the effective humanity of your program, your goals and your institutional zeal.

"Success in building publicity and awareness of a nonprofit lies in empowering and teaching nonprofit staff how the media works and how to build 'contracts' with them that grow your credibility and stature."

Source: Ann Higgins, President, Utopia Media Enhancement Services, Red Bank, NJ. Phone (732) 784-1807. E-mail: ann@utopiacommunications.biz

Media Likes Feel-good Stories

The work of nonprofits is to learn how to package stories in ways that capture media attention.

"Nonprofits need to realize that the small and wondrous achievements of their work offer the media a product they want to deliver," says Higgins. "The stories of nonprofit achievements are of human progress and victory over struggle and hope. There is not an editor, reporter or writer in the world who doesn't want those kinds of stories."

Adults in the post-9/11 world are constantly searching for affirmation about what's right. "More and more media need and demand thoughtful ideas, interviews, people and stories that restore a bit of that childhood magic," Higgins says.

Here are ideas for packaging stories:

- Media prefer a first-person account rather than a press release about recognitions.

- "For a charity to convey its mission and highlight an employee, they need to present the story to the media in a way that lets them see the employee in action," Higgins says.

- "Offer a reporter the opportunity to spend a 'day in the life of' a particular worker/volunteer. Let them see firsthand how the individual impacts the lives of the people the nonprofit serves," says Higgins.

71 Asking 'How Did I Do?' Can Save Time and Effort

Want a surefire way to leave every person who calls you satisfied?

Just ask them.

When you begin any phone call, try to ascertain specifically what that person needs from you. Over the course of the call, try to stick to that subject and meet the caller's needs to the best of your ability. At the end of the call say, "When you called you said you needed me to help you with X. Did I do that?"

Following this simple script makes people feel heard

and gives them the opportunity to correct the situation if they are not satisfied.

This technique may initially leave you feeling as if you are inviting trouble or taking more time than is necessary for the call. However, this technique will in fact end up saving time (and perhaps face) in the long run by making sure you are solving the problem the first time.

This technique will also save you time and the caller frustration by helping determine early on if you are the person who can help with his or her request.

72 Avoid Common Mistakes With Media

Is your nonprofit struggling to receive media coverage? If so, Jane Praeger, president, Ovid Inc. (New York, NY), says it could be because you have fallen prey to common mistakes nonprofits make when working with the press.

"One of the biggest problems nonprofits have in reaching the media is they pitch programs, services and organizations, instead of stories," says Praeger. "People who work at nonprofits are so passionately committed to the issues, they often become frustrated when the press doesn't share their interest or enthusiasm."

Praeger says nonprofits need a better understanding of what constitutes a story for a particular newspaper, magazine, TV show or radio program. "Awards dinners, fundraising events, programs and services, no matter how worthy, tend to draw a 'ho-hum' from journalists," Praeger says.

Instead of alerting the media of every awards dinner and fundraising event, ask: "Is this an event that offers something timely, newsworthy, fresh, surprising, unpredictable and authentic?"

"A good feature story is generally about ordinary people who, against all odds, manage to accomplish something significant. That may happen within the context of a particular program or organization, but the individual's story is the hook."

Praeger says nonprofits also have the tendency to make common mistakes during media interviews. Instead of spending extra time and energy educating the media about an issue and not receiving recognition for yourself or your organization when the story is released, Praeger recommends the PR specialist:

• Have a strong point of view about the issue at hand.

• State that point of view in language that is so specific, colorful and evocative that it can't be paraphrased by a journalist. "Metaphors and analogies that make a complex issue immediately graspable to the public work well," Praeger says. "For TV, try to come up with quotes that are short, punchy and to the point."

Source: Jane Praeger, Ovid Inc., New York, NY. Phone (212) 929-4795. E-mail: jane@ovidinc.com

---

Replace Jargon Words

Before writing your next press release or entering your next media interview, remember to eliminate jargon from your vocabulary.

Jane Praeger, president, Ovid Inc. (New York, NY), says nonprofits tend to use jargon (e.g., community, resources, funding, outreach, underserved, marginalized, capacity-building, etc.) when speaking to the press instead of using specific terminology.

"Always look for words that are specific, concrete, simple and bring images to mind," says Praeger. "If any 10-year-old could grasp what you're saying, you're on the right track."

To replace jargon, try using basic words such as children, mothers and fathers instead of community or cash rather than funding.

"Instead of resources, describe what those resources are and what they do for people," Praeger says. "For example, instead of saying, 'We provide referrals to low-income individuals and families who may be in need of mental health services,' say, 'If people or their children are feeling anxious or sad, we make it possible for them to get help from specially trained counselors at a price they can afford.'"

73 Global Reach of Media

In the age where most media outlets have a website, new considerations arise when communicating with local media.

A media relations strategy tailored to the global reach of Web-based content is essential. The key is to remember that once something is conveyed to the media, it is most likely going to turn up in search engine results about your organization. This means every statement you make to the media has the potential to reach a global audience.

Depending on the situation you may choose to withhold information you otherwise would share simply to avoid spreading the word beyond a comfortable region. However, remember what may seem like reason for caution can also work to your advantage in certain situations. When you are specifically trying to appeal to a large audience, for a fundraising effort perhaps, the speedy spread of information across the Internet will most likely work in your favor. In cases like this it's nice to know a small article published in your town newspaper has the potential to reach a number of readers far greater than the population of the paper's delivery area.

74 Media Bank Provides Easy Access to Images

Creating a central location for your most-requested images and logos will streamline your media relations efforts and serve as a valuable resource for staff and community members alike.

At Austin Peay State University (APSU) of Clarksville, TN, "We refer all media, as well as faculty and staff wanting to use the APSU logo on department/program brochures and fliers, to the media bank when a logo or other appropriate APSU-related image is needed," says Melony A. Jones, communication specialist, public relations and marketing.

The media bank is a separate Web page (www.apsu. edu/prandpubs/media_bank/index.asp) accessible through the public relations page of the university's website. It features more than 40 images, including APSU's logo, seal and word mark, in both vector and JPEG formats; images of campus buildings and facilities; scenic campus photos and headshots of key university administrators.

Organizations with an IT department or Web designer can most likely handle design and maintenance of a media bank in-house. In APSU's case, the Web designer is in charge of updating the media bank, created using Extensis Portfolio digital asset management software. Images are updated as needed, such as when new administration takes the reign.

Password-protecting access to the media bank may be appropriate, depending on the nature of the images available. APSU currently allows both the public and the media to access all images within the media bank without the use of passwords.

"If we see our logo used incorrectly or distorted in some manner, we do contact that source because our logo is copyrighted and must be used following guidelines set by our office," says Jones.

For organizations planning a media bank, Jones recommends including logos and images the organization would like the public to see; offering at least JPEG formats of images, although other formats would be useful; and making sure images are organized.

Source: Melony A. Jones, Communication Specialist, Public Relations and Marketing, Austin Peay State University, Clarksville, TN. Phone (931) 221-7868.

75 Outreach Strategies for Rural-based Nonprofits

If your organization makes its home in a rural setting, your geographic location may restrict you to a more narrow constituency, but you also have the benefit of a captive audience.

Here are some public relations techniques useful to small-town nonprofits:

1. **Forge a positive relationship with the local media.**
   Because newspaper editors and radio news directors are more accessible than in larger cities, work to educate them on the programs of your organization and build a mutually beneficial relationship. Smaller community media outlets are continually seeking news and feature stories.

2. **Write your own news stories.** Since rural newspapers tend to have few reporters, editors will appreciate news that is already well written. Editors may print exactly what you send. Experience and the benefit of a close, comfortable relationship will help you pinpoint their preferences.

3. **Make connections with neighboring communities.**
   Reach beyond your local community by identifying human interest stories with neighboring community connections.

4. **Be a visible member of your community.** Your presence and involvement is much more noticeable and appreciated in smaller communities than larger ones. Your organization's employee involvement in local affairs is also perceived as an important benefit to local residents and community leaders.

5. **Involve media representatives in advisory capacities.**
   Appoint local editors, reporters and news directors to appropriate committees. Seek input on ways to attract regional and statewide attention.

76 Get More Mileage From Your Press Kit

Preparing media kits when you hold press conferences takes considerable time and effort, but you can extend their usefulness and even shelf life using a few of these tips:

- **Keep presentation simple.** A single binder, folder organizer with pockets or even a custom envelope helps ensure your materials will stay together when reporters are ready to write their stories. Too many pieces can make it cumbersome for most journalists' already crammed files.

- **Include attractive ready-to-use photos.** Some media attending your press conference may send writers but not photographers. Make their jobs easier by providing a high-quality selection for newspapers, TV or radio stations to use or post on their websites.

- **Add a calendar of future events.** Briefly describe each one with purpose, time, date, location, chairpersons and contact information so reporters will know in advance about upcoming newsworthy events and photo opportunities.

- **Offer brochures, newsletters and helpful background materials.** Your press kit may be designed primarily for one event, but most journalists appreciate having additional information to make their stories more complete beyond the news release you have provided. These might include brochures highlighting your recent programs and a copy of your latest newsletter.

- **Highlight your own contact information.** Choosing a folder with a business card slot is worth any minor added expense. If appropriate, prepare a roster of your department heads with their contact numbers and e-mails. Most journalists will save listings they think they may use later.

- **Remember that different media have different needs.** You may have radio, newspaper, online news services and television reporters at your press conference. Provide the basics for each of them, but consider customizing different sets of kits for each medium's needs.

77 Ideas to Maximize Publicity

Publicizing a newly launched program or service requires a plan and basic steps to which you are probably well-accustomed. Here are some ideas that go beyond the predictable steps to bring more attention:

- ❏ Ask specialty publications or area magazines to run features on your new program.

- ❏ Call in the chamber of commerce for a ribbon cutting and open house.

- ❏ Schedule live public service interviews on radio and TV.

- ❏ Call TV reporters with the promise of action video, then be sure to deliver! Offering a hands-on opportunity for a reporter — e.g., rapelling down a new climbing wall in a youth center or pulling a pan of cookies out of the oven in a new soup kitchen — can almost guarantee a fun, upbeat story that people will enjoy watching.

- ❏ Plug the new program on your website with a call to action.

- ❏ Create a club for persons who could use the service.

- ❏ Make service club presentations.

- ❏ Bake and share a cake in the shape of your project.

- ❏ Send "hometown" news releases to area newspapers where people involved in your program may live; if possible, identify residents of the small communities who use your service and, with their okay, use their names and stories to lead your news to the smalltown papers.

- ❏ Create advertising for print, radio, TV, outdoor and magazines.

- ❏ Hang banners outside a building.

- ❏ Look at your secondary audience and target messages to them.

- ❏ Plan to publicize the program repeatedly in different media.

- ❏ Tie in a fundraiser for a local charity.

- ❏ Put together a display in your organization's front lobby.

- ❏ If appropriate, ask churches, other nonprofits, businesses or the chamber to run short articles about your program in their publications.

- ❏ Remember to promote the new service well with your own employees.

78 Useful Media Sites

www.mediainfocenter.org — Managed by the Media Management Center at Northwestern University (Chicago, IL), the site provides up-to-the-minute, media-related content from authoritative global sources and 150-plus daily newspapers.

www.pathfinder.com — Links to online versions of Time, Inc. publications: Time, Fortune, CNNMoney and more.

79 Share Pearls of Communications Wisdom

"What is the most valuable piece of advice you have gotten — or you would give to other nonprofit communicators — regarding dealing with media contacts?"

"It's a two-way street: You have to keep communication channels open both to and from media contacts. It's important to build a relationship with primary contacts to establish trust. Invite them to chamber meetings as your guest, ask for their thoughts on how to best get the word out, and make as many positive 'touches' with them as possible."

— Jami M. Hornbuckle, Assistant Vice President for Communications and Marketing, Morehead State University (Morehead, KY)

"My advice to a communicator is to have worked in the media for a few years. I know that if someone is already in a communications job, these words of wisdom come a little late, but

I have seen many people come out of school with a PR emphasis who have never even worked on a college newspaper, let alone a full-time daily or weekly, or done any TV or radio work. They have no clue how these media work, how stories are assigned, how many pitches reporters and editors receive and discard every day, how newsrooms are structured, or what it is like to work under a deadline. In these cases, I see too much theory and not enough practical experience.

"The other thing is a little obvious, but it's important to learn as much about the technical side of communications as you can," from layout and design to how to shoot and edit videos and incorporate music into presentations.

— David Proctor, Director of Media and Public Relations, The Idaho Foodbank (Boise, ID)

80 Implementing a Name Change: Stay True to Mission, Services

When dealing with a name change, focus on maintaining your organization's mission while promptly communicating the news with your internal and external audiences.

In September 2007, the board of trustees at Wilmington College (New Castle, DE) approved changing its name to Wilmington University. The decision followed a two-year study by Dr. Jack P. Varsalona, president.

Suki Deen, university relations associate, says that after detailed research and approval by the board of trustees, "It was found that Wilmington College was already operating as a university by offering undergraduate and graduate degrees in a variety of different subjects, to more than 11,500 students across multiple campuses."

Preparations Include Strategy Meetings, New Ad Campaign, Website

"The university relations department worked on preparations for the name change a few months before the official announcement," says Deen. "Press releases, a new ad campaign and more were all discussed in several strategy meetings. It was important for us to work as a team to represent a fresh new image of Wilmington University."

Maintaining your organization's values and focusing on your history of success will make a name transition a smoother one, she advises.

"When moving from a college to a university, we began using more formal (type) font styles, photography and graphics. As far as content, we have tried to maintain our mission of providing student-friendly service, affordable tuition and flexible schedules at convenient locations," says Deen. "When becoming a university, we simply emphasized the qualities we already had, while introducing the new university name."

Soon after announcing the name change, they changed

the university's Web address to www.wilmu.edu. Education technology department staff

"It was important for us to work as a team to represent a fresh new image of Wilmington University."

worked to get the entire website to reflect the new name change.

In addition, signs at the main campus were changed immediately after the new name was announced, and stationary, business cards and other materials were also ordered to reflect the new name.

Be Sure to Inform Internal Audiences First

When announcing a name change, beginning with internal audiences is crucial, Deen says. "We definitely focused internally first. Dr. Varsalona first announced the name change at the college-wide meeting where he addressed the faculty and staff. Meanwhile, 50,000 letters were sent to students and alumni, advising them of the change."

The president and staff visited some classrooms to inform students firsthand.

In developing the communications strategy, she says, "We wanted the name change to be something that the Wilmington University community would be proud of. We also wanted to effectively communicate the name change, and make it clear that all questions or concerns were very much welcomed."

Deen recommends alloting at least six months prior to announcement for strategic planning. Also, make sure the top administrators/decision makers work closely with the communications department so all messages are cohesive, consistent and clear.

Source: Suki Deen, University Relations Associate, Wilmington University, Wilson Graduate Center, New Castle, DE. Phone (302) 295-1164. E-mail: suki.r.deen@wilmu.edu

81 Rules of Thumb for Listing Press Releases on Your Website

Listing press releases on your website can serve as a great resource for media contacts as well as interested community members. However, it's important to have a system for creating and updating this section so it remains a valuable, user-friendly tool.

Stacy Underwood, community development manager, Donor Network of Arizona (Phoenix, AZ), shares these tips for listing press releases on your website:

- If you're posting a press release for an event, it should be removed or moved to your archive folder as soon as the event is over.

- Post press releases about nationally recognized days that are associated with your organization.

- Provide a link to your press releases or media center on your home page.

- Time your releases with events or time of year.

- List press releases by date/newsworthiness and archived releases by year then date.

- Don't forget to include contact information on all releases.

- Check your spelling. Spell check doesn't always catch everything.

Source: Stacy Underwood, Community Development Manager, Donor Network of Arizona, Phoenix, AZ. Phone (602) 222-2215.

82 Avoid Telling a Reporter 'No Comment'

When being interviewed by the media, never respond with "no comment." While it may be just two words, it's a phrase that conveys much more in unspoken meaning.

"No comment" often can imply guilt or give the impression you have something to hide. So always have a response ready. Three alternative responses to keep in mind:

1. "By all means, we wish to address this important issue. I want to make sure I have all the facts to share with you. Please let me know your deadline and I'll get back to you before the time."

2. "It would be inappropriate for me to give an answer to that question before all the facts are in; however, when they are, you and your readers/viewers/listeners will be among the very first to know."

3. "That's a great question. And while I am not able to answer it in its entirety at this time because of ongoing discussions/pending negotiations/other specific reasons, I can tell you this:" Offer a statement of reassurance with as much detail as possible of how your organization will address/resolve the issue.

83 Minimize Negative Media Coverage

Dealing with negative media coverage is never easy. However, utilizing certain techniques will minimize the effect negative coverage has on your organization.

"Minimizing negative coverage is hard. The best defense is a good offense," says Sharon Dilling, director of marketing and communications, New Jersey Credit Union League (Highstown, NJ). "It's always a good idea to have a bank of positive undated types of stories that you can throw out at any given moment. So just after the dust settles, you can rebuild your image quickly and decisively by demonstrating your organization's value and worth. Another good offense is to be active in your community in positive ways to begin with."

Dilling shared these strategies for dealing with negative media coverage:

1. **Have one voice.** Make sure all your communication is consistent.

2. **Stay on message.** Answer your own question. Don't be led to speaking about things the reporter wants to know.

3. **Be available.** Hiding from a reporter rarely works. Be accessible even if you have to keep repeating the same 27 words to them.

4. **Know when to keep quiet.** Don't perpetuate negative news stories or keep a story going that might have died.

5. **Tell the truth.** It's hardly ever the wrongdoing, the mistake or the misstep that gets you. Most of the time, it's the cover up.

6. **Be prepared.** Don't be afraid to tell a reporter you don't know and have to get back to them. Have your statements sitting in front of you, in your wallet, on your refrigerator.

7. **Learn from past experiences of others and yourself.** Don't be afraid to admit when you messed up; just don't make the same mistakes again.

Source: Sharon Dilling, Director of Marketing and Communications, New Jersey Credit Union League, Highstown, NJ. E-mail: sdilling@njcul.org

84 Think Tank Creates Network of Advocates

Creating an online *think tank* will link supporters to one another and also provide you with an avenue to garner support for a specific cause.

"Friends of Binghamton University already know about the profound impact the university makes on students, our community and our state. The Think Tank advocacy network was created as a way to share that impact with elected officials," says Gail Glover, director of media relations, Binghamton University (Binghamton, NY).

"Once signed up as members of the network," Glover says, "think tank advocates have access to a variety of tools and resources to guarantee that their voices — and Binghamton University's value — are recognized in Albany and Washington.

"Supported by a multi-page website — Think. binghamton.edu — advocates also receive bi-monthly newsletters that feature university news, achievements and advocacy issues," says Glover. "From time to time, think tank advocates are invited to participate in advocacy activities — sending letters to elected officials and the media for example — to support the university, its mission and the value it delivers."

Launched in the fall of 2007 after five weeks of development, Binghamton's think tank has about 1,000 registered members.

"We're using a variety of methods to get people enthused enough about the project to sign up," says Glover. "We've had sign-up tables at alumni and university events and sent numerous e-mail invitations to alumni, staff, faculty and friends of the university."

The think tank — involving staff from communications, government relations and alumni offices, with guidance from senior staff and the university president — grew from a need to make more people aware of Binghamton's value and vision, and the impact it makes on students, the community and state, she says.

Content not available in this edition

The online think tank for Binghamton University promotes advocacy.

Its benefits are two-fold, says Glover: "Legislators are receiving and hearing our messages, and we are building a strong network of supporters who are informed and engaged with the university and as such, can carry our messages into a variety of arenas."

Source: Gail C. Glover, Director of Media Relations, Binghamton University, Binghamton, NY. Phone (607) 777-2174. Website: www.binghamton.edu

85 Educate Staff on Media Issues

Responding to a media inquiry in a timely manner fosters goodwill with any media outlet. To be ready to do so:

- **Let staff know who is authorized to speak to the media.** Many organizations have a specific spokesperson(s) authorized to do so. If you have more than one such person, make sure staff know the chain of command for those people and have all necessary contact information.

- **Make sure all staff have a current copy of your organization's media points.** Include general information on the organization, boilerplate answers for key questions and updated statistics and financial information.

- **Keep staff updated on sensitive issues or potential crises.** If a lawsuit is pending or a staff issue is about to erupt, make sure people know how to handle it. You may have to override your usual policies about handling media inquiries (e.g., all calls go to the CEO). Make sure everyone knows of this override.

- **Offer media training to staff and key volunteers** so they are always prepared to represent your organization and handle themselves in a professional and appropriate manner.

86 Prepare Mentally, Physically for Television Interviews

Television exposure for your organization's events and good works can mean greater public awareness and support. Using some of these techniques can help ensure that viewers focus on your message — not your hairstyle or accessories.

✓ **Be comfortable and cool.** Wear light- to medium-weight clothing free of distracting patterns or colors. Heat from studio lights may cause perspiration, and tight clothing may make you fidgety.

✓ **Eliminate noisy jewelry or accessories.** Bangle or charm bracelets can be an unwelcome distraction, especially when knocking against microphones. Remove keys and change from your pockets.

✓ **Remember appropriate attire.** A simple suit or dress works best for studio interviews, but on-site remotes from construction or rescue locations call for toned-down clothing. Keep your objective, location and message in mind when dressing.

✓ **Forget about the camera.** Find a comfortable position in your seat and focus on the interviewer while maintaining good posture, using natural hand gestures and keeping the tone conversational.

✓ **No special makeup tricks.** Women should wear normal day makeup, while men should shave shortly before the interview. Allow makeup technicians to powder shiny skin or blot perspiration if needed. Listen to their advice — remember the Kennedy-Nixon debates.

✓ **Identify and stick to your key points.** When the edited interview is aired, you won't likely have more than 30 to 90 seconds to state your case, so practice a one-minute "elevator" style pitch in the mirror until you feel comfortable and confident. Integrate your main points into every possible question.

✓ **Smile and relax.** Show enthusiasm for your cause and gratitude to supporters with a smile, keeping other gestures like nodding to a minimum. Keep your hands in your lap while sitting or by your side if standing.

87 Employ Multiple Tactics When Faced With Controversy

When dealing with controversial issues, know that some may require your communications staff to speak up, while others are better handled with silence.

Cass Cliatt, director of media relations, Princeton University (Princeton, NJ), has dealt with a number of controversial issues affecting the university. She says different tactics are necessary depending on type of controversy and amount of coverage the situation has already garnered.

When it comes to controversial or false information being printed about the university, Cliatt says media relations staff take an aggressive approach. When an article is printed containing false information, she immediately issues a release stating the correct information, and/or posts a message on Princeton's website. She stresses the importance of issuing a correction the same day the false/controversial news is aired.

In some cases, however, you can do little to combat controversy other than staying silent. While this can sometimes be misconstrued by the media, Cliatt says it is the appropriate approach in some cases, such as when dealing with an issue that may be damaging to a member of the university's community. (Universities, she notes, are often forbidden by law from commenting on issues relating to both students and alumni. In these cases, it may be worthwhile to let the media know why staff is unable to comment so they know the reason for your silence.)

Gauging whether to speak up or stay silent can be a challenge. One way to measure how you should react, Cliatt says, is to ask yourself: "Can the story continue without me?" If the story relies solely on your comments or participation, then it may be beneficial to keep quiet until the story disappears. However, if other parties are commenting about your organization, it is important to share your side of the story, preserve your organization's reputation and set the record straight.

Source: Cass Cliatt, Director of Media Relations, Princeton University, Princeton, NJ. Phone (609) 258-6108. E-mail: ccliatt@princeton.edu

88 Don't Overlook Smaller Newspapers

■ Remember to add a local angle to releases going to smaller area newspapers. They're hungry for news and will often publish more detailed news releases and photos you provide.

Here's a tip for connecting with these previously overlooked media outlets and letting them know you care about their audience: Ask your clients, board members, donors and other persons of influence where they come from, and whether their hometown community (or current place of residence) has a local paper. With the source's okay, send a news release that spotlights his/her involvement in your cause. This project is perfect for a summer intern in your office! Just provide the boilerplate news release and let the intern go to it!

89 Go Beyond 'No Comment'

Q. "Is it ever OK to say 'no comment' to the media?"

"My personal opinion is no, simply because it shuts you off from the media and leaves a negative impression. Especially into today's media, 'no comment' leaves the impression that you have something to hide, even though many times that is not the case. You can wordsmith your remarks to essentially say 'no comment' but in a more polite and/or responsive manner. Rather than saying 'no comment', you can state something to the effect of 'Because of the ongoing investigation, it is not proper for us to remark at this time on the situation. We plan to fully explore the issue and as soon as I can, I will get back to you.' Then of course, you need to follow up. Typically when you are faced with having to use the 'no comment' response it is because of a negative situation. Why add fuel to the fire? Better to respond in a friendlier manner while essentially saying the same thing."

— *Sharon Myers, Director of Communications,*
St. Joseph's Collegiate Institute (Buffalo, NY)

"There is a serious discussion in the PR community, driven by the Public Relations Society of America, about if we, as PR professionals, are duty bound to respond to all media inquiries, particularly those who have demonstrated they have an ax to grind with your organization. There are, for example, scores of online newsletters positioning themselves as 'watchdogs' over industry segments or specific organizations. Some are legit and provide a service. For many of them, however, there is nothing you can say or do to get a fair shake. They'll bombard you with rumor and innuendo, and then still report it as fact, with your answer as a 'denial.' And you can spend your entire day answering only their questions. It's very tempting to dismiss them with 'no comment.' So we have to rethink that old 'always answer all questions' philosophy against the backdrop of the emergence of new media and learn how to do what is practical and best for your organization."

— *David Morrison, Director, Communications and Publications,*
Brenau University (Gainesville, GA)

90 News Blog Invigorates Online Newsroom

Go beyond a typical blog to start a news-specific blog for your online newsroom.

"We created the Babson College news blog in March 2006," says Michael Chmura, director of public relations, Babson College (Babson Park, MA). "Different individuals gather information through different methods — some prefer text, others video and others audio. The blog reaches that audience.

"In addition, we saw the blog as a flexible tool to deliver news that doesn't fit the traditional press release format: interviews, business profiles, conference coverage, etc.," says Chmura.

"The blog allows us to distribute information immediately," he says. "We can attend a presentation and post from the room. We can liven up coverage of events, like our student business fair, with multiple photos of the teams. In many ways it serves as our mini-online daily newspaper."

Created in one day by the in-house marketing media group, the blog allows readers to access an archive of posts dating back to March 2006 and lets readers print posts or e-mail a link to the blog to a friend or colleague.

Any public relations staff member can post information on the news blog.

"The flexible and casual design of a blog gives us the freedom to publicize a greater variety of events and news about community members than we would be able to by using more traditional methods," says Chmura.

He says that so far the response to the blog has been

extremely positive and reporters are using it as a resource for story ideas.

When it comes to formatting a news blog, the options vary from posting brief updates as frequently as several times a day to posting lengthy updates less often.

"My personal preference is to post brief items on a regular basis," Chmura says. "Images, photos, logos, even clip art all help to brighten up the presentation. It is also important to offer your readers RSS feeds."

Check out the blog at: www3.babson.edu/Newsroom/blog/default.cfm.

Source: Michael Chmura, Director of Public Relations, Babson College, Babson Park, MA. Phone (781) 239-4549.

91 When Being Interviewed...

- The next time you are being interviewed by the media, stay focused on one or two key points rather than rambling. Doing so will help get your ideas across and ensure the accuracy of what is being said.

92 Seek Media Input on Your Communications Techniques

Many organizations rely on free news coverage to spread the word about upcoming events and other newsworthy items. If you haven't been receiving the coverage you are after, reach out to local media contacts to find out what you can do to make your news items more appealing and increase the chances that your events will be covered.

Consider asking local journalists to sit down for a casual interview. Bring examples of press releases and other materials with and ask for feedback. Prepare a short list of

questions regarding specifics they are looking for in press releases and story pitches.

This casual session can help identify problems on your end, such as releases that are too lengthy or directed to the wrong department. These and other simple tips from local media will give you the knowledge you need to develop materials that will be more appealing to these outlets and in turn garner your organization more coverage.

93 Pop Culture Reference Jazzes Up News Releases

Looking for a catchy title or introduction for your next press release? Look to popular culture for inspiration.

Doing so paid off for Centenary College (Hackettstown, NJ), says Annamaria Lalevee, public relations director. When the school introduced a new forensics science certificate in 2004, Lalevee played on the popularity of the TV show, *CSI* (which stands for "crime scene investigation").

Here are the news release's headline and lead paragraph:

FIND THE FIELD OF FORENSIC SCIENCE FASCINATING? CENTENARY COLLEGE NOW OFFERS A CERTIFICATE IN CRIMINALISTICS — THE ONLY CONCENTRATION OF ITS KIND IN THE COUNTRY

Hackettstown, NJ, Feb. 19, 2004 — Run to the television every time CSI is on wishing for a career that is as fascinating as the investigators on the show? Well, wish no more. Centenary College now offers two

undergraduate programs in criminalistics: one geared for the traditional student (concentration in forensic science studies) and another for the professional who is already employed in the law enforcement field (certificate in criminalistics – master forensic investigator).

"The results were great," Lalevee says of the story angle. "The Associated Press did a feature on it and it showed up in more than 25 newspapers" throughout the country, plus one in Canada, and was featured on the local CBS TV affiliate.

Lalevee recommends giving your press releases a fresh perspective with popular references from TV, film or music. She advises inserting a popular reference in the title of your press release, if applicable, to make it even more noticeable.

Source: Annamaria C. Lalevee, Public Relations Director, Centenary College, Hackettstown, NJ.
Phone (908) 852-1400, ext. 2238.
E-mail: laleveea@centenarycollege.edu

94 Check Your Media List

When faxing press releases or making follow-up calls to media, keep a detailed list of contacts you have already made. It's common for radio and television stations to be in the same building. To avoid sending duplicate press materials to the same station, cross check phone and fax numbers to make sure media outlets don't overlap.

If you keep a list of media contacts in a database, create an additional column to document when and how you made contact. If you have the time and resources to track coverage, add a column stating whether or not each outlet has done a story on your organization. This will serve as a good reference when sending future press materials.

95 Prepare for Phone Interviews

If you pitch stories to national media outlets, you may find yourself conducting frequent radio interviews via telephone.

If your communications staff has little experience with live phone interviews, consider creating a mock interview to prepare for the real thing.

Set up a seasoned interviewee to play the role of the reporter and the interview "trainee" the role of the person being interviewed. Place them in separate offices with the doors closed.

Have the "reporter" call the other staff person and treat the conversation as if this were a live interview. Have them try not to back track or start over if possible. Make sure the staff member posing as the interviewer stays in character. Aim to get through the interview a minimum of three times without having to stop.

Throw in a few "glitches" that could occur in an actual interview, realizing that the more you practice, the more prepared you will be for the unexpected.

96   Media Workshops Build Relationships With Reporters

Building mutually beneficial relationships with local media is important to every nonprofit. Establish yourself as an invaluable resource by hosting a media workshop.

April Klutenkamper, marketing director, Youth In Need (St. Charles, MO), defines a media workshop as "an educational and networking opportunity for the media to learn more about a community issue. The ultimate goal of the workshop is to provide reporters, editors and producers with information that will help them cover future stories in a comprehensive manner. You also position your organization as an 'expert' in the field."

While the workshop may not increase your media coverage in the near future, "The goal is to help media understand the nuances of a particular issue. You are the experts, which is why media seeks you out as sources for their stories. A media workshop is an opportunity to share your expertise, build relationships and establish credibility. A reporter is likely to remember you and your organization's services the next time," she explains.

Collaborate With Fellow Nonprofits

If your organization does not have sufficient resources to create a solo workshop, create a multi-organization workshop instead. "Smaller organizations, or those on a tight budget, should consider partnering with groups that provide similar services. You can plan and execute a great workshop with little cost to each organization, and you might also achieve bigger name recognition through such a partnership."

Workshop Expenses

The key costs are presentation materials and media handouts. Use simple handouts and produce the majority of the materials in-house to save time and money. "Invite reporters who cover nonprofits, health care, education, etc. Targeting the right person is key. Invitations can be produced on your agency's letterhead, so there's no need for special printing. As far as handouts, the biggest cost comes from purchasing the binders. Volunteers can help assemble the materials. Share costs with partnering organizations."

Klutenkamper says it's important for workshop hosts to follow up with workshop attendees to determine what information they found most useful and monitor subsequent media coverage.

Source: April Klutenkamper, Marketing Director, Youth In Need, St. Charles, MO. Phone (636) 946-5600, ext. 200. E-mail: aklutenkamper@youthinneed.org

Create a Workshop Binder

Klutenkamper created a take-home binder for all media attending the workshops. The binder included:

- Program agenda
- Presenters' contact information
- Topic introduction/overview
- Information about the law
- Topic details
- Topic statistics
- Key findings from pertinent studies
- Fact sheets, materials media can publish and additional resources

"All of these items are customizable to the workshop topic. All items may not apply to all topics," says Klutenkamper. "We tried to provide the essential details in the binder. If the reporters left with no other information, what would be the key things they need to know? That helped us narrow down the important points."

Look to other organizations for useful materials you can incorporate into your presentation. "For the domestic violence workshop, we reprinted a lot of the general material from the Rhode Island Coalition Against Domestic Violence, which provided the master format for our binder. They, too, did a workshop for journalists in their community," says Klutenkamper. "As the organization holding the workshop, I worked with our panelists to pull together the fact sheets. I created one about our program, and then used handouts they already had to create the pieces for their areas. Because we partnered with law enforcement and victims' services groups, they already had a lot of the statistics, etc. that we would need. The key is to not recreate the wheel. Use your experts on staff to get the material together. Then, the marketing staff can handle the physical presentation of the materials."

Klutenkamper also shares these ideas for what to include in a presentation binder, saying, "Finally, I would say nonprofits should be sure to include the contact information for all the experts who present at the workshop. Each reporter should also leave with an overview of the nonprofits' services, the PR contact there and a general overview of the topic. Instead of a binder, this information could also be organized easily in a three-pronged pocket folder, etc. Feel free to do it on a smaller scale and in a way that meets your budget. But each reporter should definitely leave with something."

Workshop Advice

Klutenkamper shares tips for creating a successful workshop:

1. Pick a topic in which your agency specializes.
2. Plan your hour-long program around that topic. Select staff to speak on different aspects of the issue. Partner with other agencies or groups to create a panel of experts for the topic.
3. Provide valuable topic handouts and speaker contact information. Reporters will use your reference guide the next time they cover the issue.
4. Send invitations to local area media. Be sure to follow up with phone calls.
5. Provide light refreshments.
6. Offer reporters an opportunity to ask the panelists or presenters questions.
7. Follow up with those who could not attend by mailing the binder with a letter summarizing what was covered.

97 When to Invite the Media And Set Up the Podium

"What news situations warrant a press conference?"

"A press conference is a good way to bring life to news that would normally not get much pick-up by TV," says Funda Alp, director of communications, Sacred Heart University (Fairfield, CT). "The visual aspect of the conference can make the news more interesting to a TV audience."

Alp details three situations in which a press conference is warranted:

- **To convey important news, fast.** "Press conferences are often the best way to convey important news and information in the event of an emergency. They are usually the best way to get important information out quickly under otherwise difficult circumstances."

- **To shine the spotlight on a big name.** "If you are promoting an event with a celebrity or are making an announcement with a well-known or hard-to-access spokesperson, a press conference is a great way to give the media the opportunity to interact with someone who is typically difficult to access."

- **To share exciting news.** "Press conferences are also a great way to share important good news that will have an impact on the organization's community at large. When possible, partner with other involved organizations for a joint conference, or engage the support of local government officials who may bring more attention to the event."

Source: Funda Alp, Director of Communications, Sacred Heart University, Fairfield, CT. Phone (203) 396-8241.

99 Create Excitement For a Big Announcement

Looking to generate some excitement in advance of a big announcement? Create a countdown to unveil major developments, like an organization name change or the creation of a satellite office. Pick a start date for the countdown, perhaps one month prior to the announcement. Create a section on your website to count down the days until the big reveal with an actual countdown clock on your site that keeps ticking away until the day of the announcement. During that time, be sure to also incorporate the countdown into all outreach materials.

Creating a countdown will increase the amount of community buzz and also spark the interest of local media. The key is not to start the countdown too early, otherwise you may find it difficult to keep the momentum going.

98 Media Terminology

Delayed Lead — Writing style in which the story's specific subject doesn't come into clear focus until some time after the first paragraphs; intent is to set the background and tone before getting to the main point.

Inverted Pyramid — Style of writing in which the most comprehensive information is in the lead, followed by less-important information; constructed so an editor can cut from the bottom up and have a complete story that meets space limitations.

Media Alert — Also referred to as news advisory or tip sheet; a brief summary of basic facts surrounding an event, often used when time is short.

Official Statement — Also referred to as a position paper; a written comment prepared for the purpose of responding consistently to any question from the media regarding a particular, sometimes controversial, issue.

100 Tips for Writing An Effective News Release

Keep these important tips in mind when writing your next press release:

✓ Make the first 10 words of your release powerful, as they are the most important.

✓ Keep your release to two pages or less. On rare occasion, you can opt for a third page, if necessary, to provide critical details.

✓ Don't sell — releases that advertise get tossed. Be factual, not promotional.

✓ Provide as much contact information as possible: individual to contact, address, phone, fax, e-mail, website. The point of contact should be the person with the most information.

✓ Proofread. When you've finished your release, remember to proofread it for typographical errors. If you don't have a good eye for spelling or grammar, give the release to a friend or colleague who does. If your release looks sloppy and careless, so will you.

101 Link Your Cause to Popular Current Issues

Creating links between your organization and popular current issues is a great way to spark interest among the community and the media.

A national news story recently served as a springboard to national publicity for the United Mitochondrial Disease Foundation (Pittsburgh, PA), says Cliff Gorski, director of marketing and communications.

"We received media attention in April 2008 when the story broke that a federal vaccine court awarded a settlement to the family of a girl who suffers from autism," Gorski says. "The theory was that the vaccine may have aggravated an underlying mitochondrial disease that caused an autism spectrum disorder. It enabled us to put out a statement from our scientific advisory board and send a statement out on PR newswire from our executive director."

24-hour Lead Time Spent Crafting, Posting Statement Online

Gorski and his staff learned of the autism story through published reports detailing the family's plan to hold a news conference.

"We had roughly 24 hours to prep a statement," he says. "We wanted to be proactive, so the first thing we did was consult our scientific and medical advisory board for a statement on the matter. Once that statement was drafted, it went live on our website. We knew that once the story broke, many would go to the website first for information on mitochondrial disease, so we wanted to have helpful information there."

The day after the news conference, Gorski issued a second statement. "We referenced the autism story but were very mindful to highlight mitochondrial disease. We wanted to make sure the public understood that mitochondrial disease is a separate issue."

Fast Action Leads to National News Coverage, Tripled Web Traffic

As a result of these proactive efforts, he says, several newspapers carried the stories from the foundation, and National Public Radio interviewed the executive director.

"We work with Porter Novelli, a Washington, DC-based PR agency," Gorski says. "The minute they put our statement on PR newswire, we received calls from the Atlanta Journal Constitution, WEB MD, the Associated Press, the Baltimore Sun and other smaller regional papers. Our statement, as well as the website, was cited in each case."

> "We knew that once the story broke, many would go to (our) website first for information ... so we wanted to have helpful information there."

Website traffic tripled in the days following the story and statement posting.

React Rapidly and Choose Current Issues With Connections to Your Cause

When looking to tie current issues to your cause, target those with a direct link to the work you do, Gorski advises. Also, realize there is a limited window of opportunity in sending a statement — it should come within 24 hours of a story on a current issue.

"In our case, mitochondrial disease was mentioned many times, both when the family involved appeared on 'Larry King Live' and in their news conference. So for us it made sense to be proactive. Our call volume jumped dramatically because people were doing as we suspected they would — going to our website and seeing symptoms."

Source: Cliff Gorski, Director of Marketing and Communications, United Mitochondrial Disease Foundation, Pittsburgh, PA. Phone (412) 793-8077. Website: www.umdf.org

---

102 Three Rules for Managing Your Media Database

Chances are you have a separate database of media outlets to which you can direct news releases and other important information.

Three essential rules for managing that database:

1. **Keep your list current.** Update contact information at least quarterly. Many media outlets have high turnover, and reporters, editors and others are constantly being shuffled.

2. **Make your list segmentable,** allowing you to direct communications to targeted groups. Select only those media outlets that attract the audiences you want to reach.

3. **Learn and adhere to communications preferences.** Learn how different media outlets prefer to receive information (e.g., letter, phone, fax, videotape or e-mail).

103 Task Force Manages Extraordinary Exposure

Every organization welcomes positive media coverage. But how do you handle a news story that generates incredible exposure and becomes huge national news?

Consider creating a task force to manage media inquiries and outreach.

In September 2007, Dr. Randy Pausch, a professor at Carnegie Mellon University (Pittsburgh, PA), gave his final lecture, entitled "Really Achieving Your Childhood Dreams." It became a worldwide sensation, appearing on YouTube.com, in countless blogs, websites and newspapers, and bringing in numerous requests for copies.

"There were 760,000-plus views of multimedia pages (both hosted on cmu.edu and Google Video) and pages on www.cmu.edu related to Randy's lecture," says Marilyn Kail, assistant vice president, marketing communications. "This occurred within the course of several weeks. After the lecture itself, we had 2,500 hits to the university site; Randy had more to his personal site — in the thousands."

Quick E-mails Bring in Key Players for Task Force

To quickly and efficiently deal with the extraordinary response, the school's division of university advancement created a six-person task force. E-mails to key disciplines announcing the task force's first meeting drew representatives from marketing communications, alumni relations, media relations, development, the school of computer science and entertainment and technology center, co-founded by Pausch.

"Creating a task force to handle an interdisciplinary project is nothing new for our advancement group," says Kail. "When it became apparent that Dr. Pausch was going to appear on 'Good Morning America', 'The CBS Evening News', '20/20' and several other major TV shows, such as 'Oprah', we agreed upon the need for calling on the expertise of representatives from all of the disciplines in university advancement, along with representatives from the college of computer science, to prepare for what might be needed and the university response.

"In terms of approval, we informed our vice president of university advancement and the dean of the school of computer science (where Pausch is on the faculty) that we were assembling this group and why. They gave us the green light immediately," Kail says. "We kept our vice president and the rest of the university's senior management team updated with regular e-mails from one point person assigned to the task."

Task Force Provides Timely Responses to Public, Media Inquiries

The task force allowed the university to better respond to the large volume of requests for the speech and for interviews, says Kail. Many marketing communications staff members had experience in national consumer marketing/advertising/PR campaigns before coming to Carnegie Mellon, she notes, "so the training and experience just 'kicked in' for handling mass exposure/response."

Each task force member had specific responsibilities, such as dealing with donation inquiries, creating a special landing page, editing and creating the DVD package, keeping senior management informed and also updating Pausch and securing his approval on the latest developments and inquiries.

A page on the university's website is devoted to finding more information about the professor and his lecture, including how to view or obtain a copy.

Source: Marilyn Rossa Kail, Assistant Vice President, Marketing Communications, Carnegie Mellon University, Pittsburgh, PA. E-mail: mkail@andrew.cmu.edu

104 Assemble a Media Portfolio

Keep copies of media coverage to build a portfolio for your organization.

Request copies of media coverage, such as clips on the evening news or feature articles and photos in print publications. Most local TV stations will provide a dubbed tape for free as long as you pick it up — same goes for local radio stations.

Compiling a detailed media portfolio is a great way to illustrate your nonprofit's success and will come in handy when meeting with potential donors and employees. If you have an in-house graphic artist, consider compiling some of your media coverage into a video reel or slideshow to show at special events or important meetings.

105 Track Media Coverage

"How do you track your nonprofit's media coverage?"

"We use a clipping service to track news coverage. We have it search several key words and phrases and our name. This works well for newspapers and is reasonably priced. As a small nonprofit, we do the best we can to be aware of magazine, television and radio publicity. We rely heavily on word of mouth, hoping association friends and staff see or hear things and let us know. It's not a reliable system but because brain injury isn't as mainstream as we would like it to be, it's still a big deal to get media play and we tend to hear about it. Additionally, I subscribe to Google Alerts (www.google.com/alerts), which I find helpful in monitoring the stories that are getting media attention on brain injury."

— Caroline Leipf, Communications Associate, Brain Injury Association of New Jersey (Edison, NJ)

106 Writing a News Release? Avoid Common Mistakes

News releases continue to be a reliable, efficient way to share information with media contacts. However, a poorly constructed news release can do more harm than good. To help guarantee the right people read — and act upon — your news releases, ask these questions when drafting news releases, advises Jeffrey Bierig, director, media relations, Illinois Institute of Technology (Chicago, IL):

1. **Is there *news value* in this news release?** Make sure your news release contains actual news. Who? What? When? Where? Why? How? The answers to these questions must be in your release.

2. **Do I have a compelling headline/subject line and first paragraph?** The e-mail subject line or headline must get the reader's attention. After that, the first few sentences must keep their attention. If not, the reader will not read the entire release.

3. **Am I disseminating the news release in the manner that is best-received?** Most news releases today are sent by e-mail. Make sure that the reporter you are dealing with wants it that way. If not, make sure you are sending it the way he/she wants it.

4. **Is the recipient interested in the subject?** For example, if sending a news release about a business trend in the food industry, you will likely want a reporter who covers the food business, not a food critic.

5. **Have I embedded the news release text in the e-mail message body rather than attach it?** Always embed your news release into the body of the e-mail. Do not send your release as an attachment. Photos and other artwork are the only generally accepted attachments.

6. **Is contact information accurate?** Also, choose a contact person able to respond in a timely manner.

Source: Jeffrey D. Bierig, Director, Media Relations, Illinois Institute of Technology, Chicago, IL. Phone (312) 567-5057. E-mail: bierig@iit.edu

107 10 Media Interview Prep Tips

It's ironic but true: Looking and sounding relaxed and comfortable takes preparation. Which is especially important for a media interview.

Keep these tips in mind before an interview to get in the proper mindset:

1. Know and play to your medium. For TV, suggest visuals and activities that help complete the story. For print, come up with a graphic, photo or logo that furthers your message.

2. Relax. Stay cool. You are the expert.

3. Take the initiative.

4. Select two or three main communication goals.

5. Cover these goals early.

6. Come back to them often.

7. Don't speak off the record.

8. Be personable. Establish rapport while maintaining professionalism.

9. Correct yourself. If you think you gave a rambling answer, say so and rephrase your answer more succinctly. Reporters will most likely prefer a smooth answer anyway.

10. Give the phone number where you can be reached during the time the reporter will be writing the story.

Additionally, when talking to...

A print reporter — Don't limit questions or ask to see a story before it's printed. Take time to clarify your points. Ask if the reporter would like you to explain a point further or go over something again.

A television reporter — Dress appropriately. Look at the reporter, not the camera. Project energy and enthusiasm as you make your point in brief "sound bites." If bringing the reporter to your agency, choose a setting with an appropriate background. Bring in props, such as flowers, plants or a lamp, to soften the setting. Think "B-roll," too.

A radio reporter — Have notes to help with your answers, but don't read them word for word. Sound conversational. Remember the sound of your voice is of utmost importance, so speak clearly and with energy.

108 Website Newsroom Tip

Include a "Media Room" button on your home page that allows the media direct access to downloadable stock photos (print quality of 300 dots per inch).

109 Recognize the Need to Improve Your Press Coverage

Is it a struggle to get adequate media attention for your nonprofit?

"We are competing for the media's attention in a world filled with up-to-the-minute news. We have to be interesting, compelling and relevant. Make sure your news releases are clear and concise if you want to get the media's attention," says Laura Lessnau, associate director, University of Michigan News Service (Ann Arbor, MI).

She offers professionals the following techniques to improve press coverage:

1. **Determine your target audience.** Lessnau says, "Ask yourself: 'Am I trying to fill seats or enhance reputation?'"

2. **Get to know individual reporters and the stories they write.** "It is better to figure out who writes what so you will have more success when you send press releases. It's far better to send your release to a handful of reporters whom you know, than to a slew of media that you don't know," she says.

3. **Clarify your message** and points you are trying to make.

4. **Give the media real news** about your organization or promote a person who can say something relevant to a timely national topic. "Local media are always looking to localize a big national story. If your news is topical, put human faces behind it," says Lessnau.

5. **Write a clear news release in conversational style.** "Many reporters read a headline and first sentence and pitch the release. If you can write something simple, punchy and interesting, you will catch their attention and you are more likely to make it into their to-do pile."

6. **Anticipate the media's needs.** 1) Have high resolution photos available; 2) produce a b-roll of a program/ project for TV stations; 3) have interviewees available and open to interviews; and 4) consider media training for your leaders. "The media has a tendency to come back to the places that are easy to work with," she says. "Once you establish a reputation like that, they will be calling you."

Source: Laura Lessnau, Associate Director, University of Michigan News Service, Ann Arbor, MI. Phone (734) 647-1851. E-mail: llessnau@umich.edu

110 Focus on Unique Strengths

 "How can we create a positive reputation that would put us at the level of our competition?"

"I think the biggest reputation trap institutions and organizations fall into is trying to be all things to all people. Realistically, 99 percent of institutions and organizations will never have the reputation that, say, a Stanford, Harvard or an American Red Cross does (deserved or not). However, each of our organizations can work to become known as a 'Stanford' or 'American Red Cross' at the two to three things that they are really, really good at. Specialization, focus and refinement breed expertise, and expertise is fertile ground for building one's reputation.

"Although it takes getting over a lot of egos, if an organization can get past that and truly be honest about the very few things that make them better than competitors, they can start to move forward. This is probably the equivalent of 'Step 2' in a 12-step program: acceptance. Most people never get past Step 1, denial; as if admitting X is not their organization's strong suit will some how mean that people are content being second best or 'ordinary' in those areas!

"It's a very common problem, though; look at how various regions promote themselves as tourist destinations... 'We have hiking. We have historical sites. We have golf courses.... "My first question whenever I see those promotional resources is 'And?' Why should we visit your area over hundreds or thousands of other options? What makes you 'special?'... What can you do better than almost anyone else?

"Once those types of questions have been answered, and the staff and board are willing to undergo a reality check, then an institution or organization is ready to move forward and become known as 'the' place to be for X."

— *Derek Tonn, President, mapformation, (Springfield, MN)*

---

111 Media Tip to Share With Your Employees

To avoid having your colleagues surprised by an unexpected call from a reporter, instruct them to be prepared with a standard response that can buy them some time to get answers or collect their thoughts: "I'm pressed for time at the moment, but I would be willing to call you back with a response."

112 When The News Comes to You: Hosting Political Candidates

When a presidential campaign is in full swing, stories about candidates garner top billing. So how do you capitalize on this when the candidates come to your doorstep?

With skillful collaboration and strategic planning, says Philip Terranova, vice president, university relations, Drexel University (Philadelphia, PA). The university hosted seven Democratic presidential candidates for a live MSNBC debate Oct. 30, 2007.

"We had heard that the Democratic National Committee (DNC) was looking to hold a debate in Philadelphia," Terranova says. "NBC called to request a site visit. NBC subsequently made two more visits to campus and then we were informed that Drexel had been selected as the host venue."

With five weeks' lead time, "our office of government and community relations began planning immediately," he says. Planning also involved university relations, the facilities department, public safety and parking departments.

"Political candidates merit and require equal treatment in all regards," Terranova says. "Hosting a field of seven candidates meant providing equal but separate holding rooms, parking and accommodations for their representatives. That two of the candidates required Secret Service involvement added complexity. Also, with the presence of three standing state governors and a mayor, security was a key consideration."

TV Network Hosting Event Plays Key Role, Absorbs Major Costs

MSNBC officials played an integral role, Terranova says. "As an MSNBC event, the network had its own security team, which worked with Drexel's public safety department as well as the Secret Service, Pennsylvania State Police and the Philadelphia Police Department. All of the production costs, including building out the stage of our main building auditorium to enlarge it, were covered by MSNBC."

Students Recruited, Trained to Accommodate Journalists, Media Teams

In addition to MSNBC crew and equipment, the debate drew more than 400 journalists. Drexel officials recruited and trained 300 student volunteers to work with media, answer questions about the campus and city, assist with parking directions, check on equipment needs, distribute materials, assist with credentialing and other needs.

"Having the candidates at Drexel was an overwhelmingly positive experience for the entire university community," says Terranova. "The great challenge was to execute a quality experience for all stakeholders in the debate... without disrupting the ongoing Drexel enterprise. We succeeded in keeping all of our core commitments to students, faculty, staff and visitors while at the same time coordinating complex debate-related logistics that encompassed at least 10 campus locations.

"A well-defined division of labor is essential because a debate is a collaboration involving the host institution, the DNC and the television network," he says. "This core work group then interacts with a host of federal and municipal agencies and other stakeholders including, of course, candidates' representatives. Drexel's office of government and community relations, led by Vice President Brian Keech, did a masterful job of coordinating the interaction among the various agencies involved in the preparation of the event."

Source: Philip Terranova, Vice President, University Relations, Drexel University, Philadelphia, PA. Phone (215) 895-2613.

113 Be Thorough, Detailed in Press Releases

The more information you include in press releases, the less time you will spend following up with media inquiries.

News releases from The Omaha Symphony (Omaha, NE) often include information about photo and video opportunities, says Lex Poppens, vice president, marketing.

"I prefer that we give members of the media as much information as possible in as short a time as possible," says Poppens. "If they know up front that this is a resource for them, they can plan their piece content better... Our public relations manager comes from the media side and knows that the shortest distance between the pitch and actual column inches is accessibility."

Other information to consider including: interview opportunities and access information, such as whether a media pass is needed to enter certain areas of an event.

Source: Lex Poppens, VP, Marketing, The Omaha Symphony, Omaha, NE. Phone (402) 342-3836, ext. 127.
E-mail: LPoppens@omahasymphony.org

114 Media Reports Illustrate Outreach Effectiveness

Tracking your news coverage and compiling it into an extensive media report will serve to further your media relations efforts.

At Hamline University (Saint Paul, MN), "we track all of our news coverage, and compare our coverage in the major papers to that of other local private universities," says JacQueline Getty, media relations director. "We use this to get a sense of the scope of our coverage, where we need to refocus our pitching efforts, and whether we are hitting our earned media outreach goals."

Use Various Sources to Track Media Coverage

"We collect the information as it hits the media, through Google searches and through e-mails from a broadcast clipping service we work with."

Hamline's media relations department (one full-time staff member and two part-time interns) creates the media reports, posts a modified version — a running list of all media coverage garnered — on its website and e-mails the reports in Microsoft Word documents to roughly 50 leaders within the organization.

"The media report includes metrics on where Hamline is garnering coverage, along with the advertising value of that coverage and the number of people the coverage is reaching," Getty says. "We also choose the top five to 10 placements and include that in the report. In addition, we do a clip comparison of stories that have run in the major Twin Cities newspapers: the *Star Tribune* and the *St. Paul Pioneer Press*. In that document we compare the number of positive and negative stories and headlines to those of 15 other private colleges and universities in Minnesota. The entire quarterly reports are typically three or four pages long."

Realize That Time Spent Compiling Reports Is Time Well-invested

Compiling a report of this magnitude will take a considerable amount of time, but it is time well-invested, Getty says. Still, some organizations may prefer to create media reports more or less frequently depending on staff availability and amount of coverage typically received. In Hamline's case, she estimates they spend two hours a week compiling media clips and five hours a week entering metric data on clips (inches of copy, dollar value, audience size, etc.) Clip comparisons are done monthly, taking about six hours to compile, and quarterly reports take about four hours to complete.

While the university uses a clipping service, there are ways to gather news coverage without paying for a service. "Google and other search engines are an excellent way to track coverage of your organization," says Getty. "We search our local news sites — MinnPost.com, a new online newspaper that is growing in popularity, in addition to all

of our local television and radio sites, as their stories do not typically pop up in Google searches. We also use WestLaw.com to do the clip comparisons between Hamline and the other universities."

Bring Staff, Colleagues in on Search for Media Coverage

Another important component of assembling comprehensive media reports, Getty says, is to remind your staff and colleagues to alert your media relations team if they are interviewed or come across coverage of your organization: "We ask our professors and experts to contact us whenever they have been contacted by the media so that we can help them coordinate the interview, and also so that we are aware of it and can run the clip later."

Media reports can provide your organization with the information needed to make modifications to your media outreach and help determine what efforts have been the most successful, she says. "It's important to know how people are talking about your organization. We can look at our data and ask ourselves important questions like: Are we doing everything we can be doing to educate people about what we have to offer? Are we using our resources wisely to promote what we need to promote? Where do we need to make headway?"

Source: JacQueline Getty, Media Relations Director, Hamline University, St. Paul, MN. Phone (651) 523-2475. E-mail: jgetty01@hamline.edu

---

115 Alert Media Contacts Of Communications Staff Changes

Whether your communications director is leaving or you are adding to your media relations staff, don't assume media contacts will notice the new name on your website or press release. Communicate staff changes immediately to avoid any confusion.

Such changes are opportunities for new staff to introduce themselves and establish rapport with journalists. Giving media contacts the heads-up about an important media-related staff change also helps guarantee your organization won't miss out on news coverage because media contacts were unable to find the right person to interview — particularly important when dealing with media contacts who regularly cover issues effecting your organization or with whom you have a close working relationship.

Lightning Source UK Ltd.
Milton Keynes UK
UKOW012319110713

213588UK00006BA/264/P